Please

CARRY ME

LORD

Please

CARRY ME
LORD

Rose Cornelsen

Kindred Press

Winnipeg, MB, Canada   Hillsboro, KS, USA

Please Carry Me Lord

Copyright © 1989 by Kindred Press, Winnipeg, MB

Jointly sponsored by the Evangelical Mennonite Conference, Steinbach, Manitoba and the Mennonite Brethren Board of Christian Literature, Winnipeg, Manitoba

Published simultaneously by Kindred Press, Winnipeg, MB R2L 2E5 and Kindred Press, Hillsboro, Kansas 67063

Cover Design by Lee Toews, TS Design Associates, Winnipeg, Manitoba

Printed in Canada by Derksen Printers, Steinbach, Manitoba

International Standard Book Number: 0-919797-91-1

Acknowledgements

Special thanks to the Evangelical Mennonite Conference and Kindred Press for the faith you have shown in me by publishing my manuscript. I feel indebted to Gilbert Brandt, Debra Esau and Lorraine Cornelsen for typing, editing and making the book readable. Special thanks also to Betty Barkman for her continual support and encouragement.

I am deeply grateful for the friendship of Rhonda McRorie who persistently inspired me to move on. Her production of the musical drama, "Better Tomorrows," based on our story, truly blessed our family. Thanks to the whole drama crew!

Through my husband's involvement with the Mennonite Disaster Service, this organization became a great source of encouragement to our family. Thank-you, everyone!

I'd like to express openly my heartfelt appreciation to Dr. Peter Kirk and Dr. Norman Hill, as well as all the other doctors, nurses and technicians who were involved in caring for our daughter during her illness. We have used pseudonyms for the doctors and the faith healer named in this story.

A special thanks to Dr. John White for allowing me to relate the profound experience we had with him. May God bless your ministry!

Without the supportive love and prayers of our caring church family we would have lost our way. You played an important role in the progression of this book. For this we are grateful.

To my mother, sisters, brothers, all my in-laws, nieces and nephews, and a very special friend, Anne Hildebrand, thank-you. You wept through our pains with us, you helped us in every practical way, and then you also laughed with us in our joys. We have been blessed by you.

Art, my husband; and children Cam, Pam and Arlene, are my most treasured inspirations. You are allowing me to share some of your most intimate experiences. I pray that God will

v

reward you with His richest blessings. I love you for your willing cooperation.

It is with deep reverence that I quote Jude 24, 25: "Now unto Him that is able to keep you from falling, and to present you faultless before the presence of His glory with exceeding joy, to the only wise God, our Saviour, be glory and majesty, dominion and power, both now and ever. Amen."

Preface

I have asked myself countless times why I am writing this book. As I prepare the final draft I have doubts and I am tempted to discard it all. It is indeed difficult to reveal facets of my life as well as of my family's; to make ourselves vulnerable to outside scrutiny. However, with the encouragement of my family and many dear friends, I place this book into the hands of my publisher, although with some trepidation.

It is my deepest desire that these pages will be a help to those in need of comfort and strength during times of sickness and grief. If my words can direct someone's anxious thoughts toward God's peace and comfort, or if feelings of weakness and inadequacy can be strengthened and fulfilled in Christ, then the glory shall return to Him and my goal shall have been reached. With that in mind I can joyfully have these words distributed throughout the whole world!

Rose Cornelsen

Dedication

This book is dedicated in appreciation to my family:

My husband Art, for your willingness to always be there for me with love, faith and encouragement.

My daughter Arlene, for your courage, optimism and depth of understanding that is so inspiring.

My son Cam, for your courage and constancy in your fight against such formidable odds.

My daughter-in-law Pam, for your quiet, loving presence that has comforted us beyond expression.

My grandson Curtis, for your boundless affection and enthusiasm that never fails to brighten my day.

My grandson Craig, for your precious reminder to us of hope, our Rainbow.

TABLE OF CONTENTS

Chapter One

CANCER !

Lying in my white hospital bed on a wintry Sunday morning, I was indulging in a bout of self-pity. The doctor interrupted with his class of interns making their daily rounds.

Pushing aside the curtains, the doctor greeted me with a cheerful, "Good morning, how are you?" He eyed me curiously but decided to ignore my tears and ran a continuous lecture for his students as they examined my surgical incision. When the group moved on to the next room my doctor stayed back.

"Has anyone told you the good news?" he asked me.

"What good news?"

"Oh, I thought my partner would have told you. Tests show that your cancer has not spread to any lymph nodes. We got it all. You have an excellent chance to be completely cured."

"Oh, thank God!" was all I could manage to respond. I had been told I would get the results the next day and had arranged for my husband to be there when the doctor came. I was taken by complete surprise. The doctor seemed hesitant to leave, as though waiting for me to say something.

"Thank you, Dr. Morgan. I wasn't expecting the results till tomorrow, but I sure needed the news today. Thanks for all you've done. I've gotten excellent care here."

"You've been a good patient and if all goes well you can probably go home in two or three days," he smiled, and with a pat on my hand he left the room. I wondered if he realized the joy he had brought into that drab hospital room that morning. Could he realize how his visit had transformed my dismal depression into new hope?

My thoughts went back to the events of the past few weeks, even the past six months. So much had happened it was

1

difficult to say when it all started. In the fall of 1981 we rushed through our harvest so as to prepare for our son's wedding on October 3. Cam's marriage to Janet Rempel would take place in Mission, BC, Janet's hometown. Just a week before leaving home, I discovered a lump in my breast and made a quick visit to my family doctor. He relieved my mind completely, suggesting the lump was merely a swollen milk gland. Amid the excitement of the wedding, the busyness of helping the couple set up housekeeping just half a mile from our farm, and getting to know our new daughter-in-law, I tried to forget about the lump. However, its very presence made peace of mind impossible and a nagging fear drove me back to the doctor in January. He did a lumpectomy and told me to go home and not to worry. I did just as I was told!

Two weeks later, our 18-year old daughter Lynette and I were enjoying a quiet afternoon at home, sipping coffee and chatting. She was in her final year at high school and we loved to talk and dream about her plans for the coming year. We were distracted from our conversation by the phone ringing. I answered the phone and my body tensed at what I heard.

"This is the surgeon from your hospital calling. It seems that the biopsy on your lump tested malignant and you're slated for a mastectomy next week!" With that pronouncement, our family was thrown into a chaos that was to plague us for years.

I could literally taste the fear that came over me. After making an appointment with the surgeon to set a hospital date, I numbly hung up the receiver.

"There must be a mistake!"

Suddenly the cozy, peaceful afternoon changed into a grey, cold twilight. Lynette's big blue eyes widened anxiously, "What's wrong, Mom?"

"Just cancer. They just tell me I have cancer, that's all!" I threw out with sarcasm. Shock and pain filled her eyes.

"Oh Lynette, I'm sorry. That wasn't fair. I shouldn't have said it like that!"

Amidst the pain of dealing with the trauma myself, I realized the need of softening the shock for the rest of the family. I decided not to tell our younger daughter when she came from school — not until I had told my husband, Art.

While waiting for Art to come home I struggled for some peace of mind.

"God," I prayed, "Dear God, you are supposed to come through at a time like this. Where are you? Say something - where is your comfort now?"

Like a flash I knew I had to let God speak to me through his Word. The Bible, of course. But where would I find what I needed? At random the Bible opened to Psalm 116.

I read it but the words did not fully register in my numbed mind. Nevertheless, the first verses somehow had a calming effect and my panic subsided somewhat.

> Psalm 116: 1-4 LB I love the Lord because he hears my prayers and answers them. Because he bends down and listens I will pray as long as I breathe. Death stared me in the face — I was frightened and sad. Then I cried, "Lord, save me."

An hour later, in the privacy of our bedroom, I was able to explain calmly to Art the events of the afternoon. My husband, a husky six-footer who prides himself in being strong, held me tight and cried. Ten years ago Art's brother had lost his wife after a two-year bout with breast cancer, and the ominous possibilities were all too real for us. After reading Psalm 116 and praying together, we were able to control our feelings enough to attend a family birthday party that had been planned for Art's sister that evening.

Upon returning home we told our children the news. We tried to break it to them gently but their silence revealed their shock, too. It was Cam who finally spoke.

"This is totally unfair. It should not happen to you, Mom. Why our family?" He sounded angry.

"I guess everybody says that Cam, " I replied.

"But. . . " He didn't finish the sentence but turned away to hide the threatening tears. I could see fear growing in the girls' eyes as well.

Art and I talked late into the night. Our twenty-one years of marriage had been all we dreamed of — ups and downs, yes, but always undergirded by love. We had had a real closeness, very little sickness, and enough prosperity to enjoy our family life. What would illness do to our well structured family life? Would we cope? We decided to try and keep our family activities as normal as possible. Psalm 116:5 reminded us that the Lord is kind, merciful and good. Surely we could trust him to work this situation into something good!

When I began to share my problem with other family members and a few friends the next day, I felt a strength flow into me as they hugged me, assuring me of their love and concern. They promised to uphold us in prayer.

Our assistant pastor and his wife, Melvin and Anne Dueck, were close friends of our family. As they came over that evening, our children gathered together with us. Before they left, Melvin reminded me of a scripture passage of James 5:14-16.

> Is anyone among you sick? Let him call for the elders of the church and let them pray over him, anointing him with oil in the name of the Lord, and the prayer, offered in faith, will restore the one who is sick, and the Lord will raise him up, and if he has committed any sins they will be forgiven him.
>
> Therefore, confess your sins to one another and pray for one another so that you may be healed. The effective fervent prayer of a righteous man availeth much.

Anointing with oil! Confessing sin! We hadn't even thought of it! Confessing sin, what did that have to do with cancer? I wanted the anointing for healing, but it seemed there might be hidden sin in my life that needed confessing. Immediately, the Lord brought to mind an incident where a Christian brother had insulted me in public but had never apologized. I thought I had forgiven him, but now the Lord showed me I was still harboring a grudge against him.

We knelt, holding hands as I openly confessed my sin. Melvin anointed me with oil and laid his hands on my head as he prayed for my healing. I wondered whether my healing would be physical, spiritual, or emotional, or all three, but I knew I wanted whatever help was available.

After the quiet anointing, a deep, settling peace came to me for the first time in two days. I knew I would sleep that night and I did! I had a deep inner joy and contentment to know that God makes no mistakes. God had proven that His strength was made perfect in my weakness.

> The Lord protects the simple and childlike, I was facing death and then he saved me. Psalm 116:6

To me, being admitted into hospital was a fearful prospect. I hated the sight of sickness, the smell of antiseptics, and I felt the claustrophobia of walls closing in on me. The most difficult aspect, however, was being strong for my children, and trying to comfort and reassure them the evening before my surgery. I almost broke down when our youngest, 13-year old Arlene, hung on and sobbed. What a blessing it was for us when God sent our pastor and his wife to pray with us that bitterly cold and stormy January evening.

After everybody left that night I sat a long time staring out of my hospital window. The St. Boniface Hospital is situated on the east bank of the Red River, and from where I sat I looked west toward the traffic crossing over the Norwood Bridge to

Main Street. Twinkling colored lights lit up the darkness, and in the strangeness of my surroundings the city became a fantasy land with the castle-like Fort Garry Hotel to my right and the never-ending flame of the Golden Boy ·atop the legislative buildings to my left. How unreal! And strangely, I was at peace! I took out a pen, to put my thoughts on paper in a letter to Art.

The modified radical mastectomy went ahead as scheduled the next morning. When I awoke, Art was there to hold my hand. I groaned as I sensed how flat my chest was even before I touched it. Art kept reassuring me he would always love me just the same as before. My arm was stiff and sore, but the incision was completely numb and painless. The full results and further treatment plans would not be available for a week; in the meantime, I would have to concentrate on gaining my strength back and exercising my arm.

On the Sunday morning five days after surgery, I was depressed. Our daughter-in-law was going to be baptized that day and our family had joyfully anticipated sharing the occasion with her. Hospitalized and unable to witness this momentous event, I had been more than a little dejected. The doctor's unexpected relay of good news, however, had wonderfully banished the gloom. Now I could hardly wait for the family to come in that afternoon!

When Art arrived, so handsomely dressed in his best navy pin-striped suit, he was carrying a gorgeous bouquet of roses. Handing me the roses, he gave me a hug and a kiss.

"Hi, Rose, you look great. How are you feeling?" he asked, obviously expecting me to be depressed.

"Wonderful! You look fantastic yourself. Thanks for the flowers! Everything's coming up roses today!"

The rejoicing was great in Room 725 that day! I remembered Psalm 116:7

> Now I can relax. For the Lord has done
> this wonderful miracle for me. He has saved
> me from death, my eyes from tears, my feet

from stumbling. I shall live! Yes, in his presence here on earth!

Not only had the cancer not spread to the lymph nodes at all, but the cancer had been entirely removed in the biopsy. There was not enough specimen left to test what treatment I should have as a precautionary follow-up. This resulted in a specific answer to prayer that I would not need any chemotherapy. I also had very little pain after the surgery and I was pronounced cured exactly four weeks later!

Throughout the trying days before surgery and for a long time afterward, I frequently asked, "Why me?" An answer would always flash back, "Why not you? It happens to others, why shouldn't it happen to you?"

One night when I lay half awake I was vividly reminded of Christ's suffering in the Garden of Gethsemane, when he begged the Father to remove the bitter cup and it was denied Him. Why should I not suffer a little bit when Jesus had suffered so bitterly for me? Could I not trust Him to see me through whatever lay ahead, even if it meant years of pain? Indescribable love and peace washed over me as I lay there, praying, "Not my will, but Thine be done." I found that praying in Jesus' name is to submit my will to His will - trusting my life into His care.

My bout with cancer taught me many precious truths. God upholds his children through trying times. There is tremendous power in His Word! I was amazed at the number of Christians, strangers as well as friends, who shared Scripture verses and prayed with me, strengthening me emotionally. Little could we realize how much more strength we would need in the years just ahead.

Chapter Two

GROWING UP

It was a cold, blustery night in February, 1938. In the tiny prairie village of McTavish, Manitoba, snow piled high outside the cottage window and Dad had to step up on a chair to look out. Hearing the moans from the bedroom he was becoming very anxious. Finally, after hours of waiting, Dad opened the door for the doctor who rushed in, just barely in time to deliver the impatient baby girl. The five older children had been bundled up and taken over to the neighbor's house. In the morning they were brought back again to welcome their brand new dark-haired baby sister named Roseline (little Rose), and to wonder about the confusing mysteries of stork-delivered babies that involved doctors.

In the next eight years, five more brothers and sisters were ushered into the family. Eking out a living for the family became a scramble for existence. Although our parents were constantly worrying about making ends meet, life was anything but monotonous for me. With five older and five younger siblings, there was never a dull moment.

Of all the family, my closest friend was Margaret, two years my junior. She was my opposite in many ways. Her easygoing and fun-loving nature contrasted my serious-mindedness. Where I was quiet and shy, Margaret was outgoing and a ready talker. Her blonde, short and bobbed hair was more flamboyant than the dark brown, long pigtails I wore. Although we were both petite, my sister was considered frail and thus not allowed to begin school until seven-and-a-half years of age. Where I found my studies difficult, however, she was to fly through them easily. We had great times together: playing, fighting, laughing, dreaming, sharing everything.

We were blessed as a loving, closely-knit family who worked and played together. When we could not afford the things many people take for granted, we learned to do without. The simple things in life brought us enjoyment, such as a special outing, hiking along the Morris River, and discovering crayfish mounds in the muddy banks. Birthdays were an opportunity to make each family member feel special, when a cake was baked and homemade ice cream made. Each of us was assigned daily chores, and we all worked in the spacious garden which supplied us with most of our staple foods, including the tons of potatoes that we devoured every year.

Our family loved singing together. Dad bought an old pump organ which my older sister, Elly, taught herself to play. Frequently Dad would gather the whole family around the organ, and we would sing our way through the hymn book! Even after family members grew up, married and left home, we sisters would still get together to sing. Our voices harmonized well, and we sang in three- and four- part harmony. Singing cemented our family relationships and helped us all become close friends. Singing was also a way to serve God, worship Him and express our love for Him and serve Him.

As long as I can remember, God has been an important part of my life. I was always aware that He was to be obeyed. As a child, I was taught that either a person was good and went to heaven when he died, or else he was bad and went to hell. Being of an overly sensitive nature, I tried unsuccessfully to be a perfect child and frequently worried about not making it to heaven. I also felt rather lost and anonymous as a middle child in a large family, with Mother and older siblings too busy to notice such emotional needs.

When I was eleven, Mom had difficulties with another pregnancy. She was nearing the time of delivery when she began hemorrhaging and was rushed to the St. Boniface Hospital, 50 miles away. I was petrified! Sleep was slow in coming that night but I must have been dozing when I suddenly awoke to the sound of uncontrollable giggling in the living room. Bewildered, I stumbled into the living room and gradually became aware of people crowding into the kitchen. With alarm, I learned that all our aunts and uncles had come to keep us company while Mom was dying! My older sisters, although under nervous strain all day, nevertheless did not fully understand the seriousness of our mother's condition and thought the relatives' concern grossly overdone. They burst into wild gales of laughter, laughing until their sides ached and they finally broke down crying.

Fearfully I prayed, "Dear God, I'm scared. I promise you my whole life if you'll just make Mom well again. Please! Please!"

That night Mom gave birth to a stillborn child. Her own life hung on a fragile thread for several days before the doctor was confident of her recovery. As a result of this incident I was assured of two things: I belonged to God, and He had answered my prayers!

A few years later, when I was 12, I attended an evangelistic service in our church. The speaker explained that "being good" alone would not get us into heaven. Our very best was like filthy rags when compared to the righteousness of God. God loved us so much that He sent His own Son Jesus Christ, into this world to save us. The only way to get to heaven was through Jesus Christ who had died to take the punishment of our sins. If we asked God to forgive our sins because of what Jesus had done, He would do it and we would be saved. When the altar call was given, I knew my time had come to make a public confession. I had no phenomenal experience, only a quiet confidence that I was doing the right thing. I stepped into the aisle and made my way to the front of the church. I was at peace with God as I knelt and accepted Him as my Savior and Lord.

In the ensuing teenage years, however, I became profoundly disturbed. Because I lacked self-confidence I allowed my mind to dwell on my ugliness, clumsiness, shyness, and every other negative self-perception that the devil held out to me. My emotional system overloaded, I would lie awake at night, fearing the dark. Nobody in the family noticed my state of mind because I was so very careful to hide it.

I was unable to express my troubled thoughts to anyone, fearing I'd be misunderstood and laughed at. I began to look for my own answers. If God is for real, surely He would understand my feelings. I began to spend more time with my Bible. I would look up and study every verse I could find on strength and comfort and peace. The book of Philippians, especially chapter four, became my refuge. With the Bible so full of promises, I knew that God in His love had a special place in His heart for me. As my precious fellowship with the Lord continued, I began to relax and gain confidence in my self-worth, and the complete nervous breakdown that I feared did not happen. I was learning to discipline my mind according to 2 Corinthians 10:5, which says we should take all thoughts captive into obedience to Christ. Philippians 4: 4-8 gave me the keys to peace of mind.

> Always be full of joy in the Lord, I say it again, rejoice! Let everyone see that you are unselfish and considerate in all you do.
> Remember that the Lord is coming soon. Don't worry about anything; instead pray about everything, tell God your needs and don't forget to thank him for his answers. If you do this you will experience God's peace which is far more wonderful than the human mind can understand. His peace will keep your hearts and thoughts quiet and at rest as you trust in Christ Jesus. Fix your thoughts on what is true and good and right. Think about all you can praise God for and be glad about.

When anxious thoughts threatened to throw me into a panic, I disciplined myself to dwell on things that were true, honorable, right, pure, lovely, respectable and good. As I would pray and confess to God that in His strength I could do anything,

I would feel His peace pervade my being. I was learning to keep my mind on Christ. I discovered I could rely on Him to keep me.

Chapter Three

COURTSHIP AND MARRIAGE

"Want to go to the beach Sunday?"

I looked up from the sack of sugar I was bagging into smaller containers. I had a clerking job at my brother-in-law's grocery store and loved it. The grocery business was suffering from the competition of the larger co-op store across the street but it was a great place for the young guys to drop in for a coke and chocolate bar.

"You want to go to the beach with our gang, Rose?"

I recognized the handsome young fellow as the son of a local farmer, but I did not know him personally. We had grown up in the same community but had attended school in different districts. I could not believe what I was hearing. I was getting used to the teasing from the guys, but there was a tone of sincerity in this fellow's voice.

"I don't think so — no — I can't."

"Why not? Don't you like me?" He was grinning as he paid for his coke. So he was only teasing after all. Just as well, I thought. Was he ever good-looking: tall, with blondish hair neatly combed back into an Elvis-style ducktail. I went back to my work, but from the corner of my eye I watched him finish his soft drink and leave the store.

The next morning he was back.

"Hi, Rosie. Well, are you going to the beach with me?"

"Good morning, Art! I thought I answered that question yesterday! No, I can't go."

"Why not?"

How could I tell him that I could not date a non-Christian, which I knew he was? I would be totally uncomfortable in a large group of unsaved teenagers.

"Just because!"

"Would you come with me to a Brunk meeting?" His soft blue eyes were so appealing!

Surprised, I looked to see if he was still teasing. Art, an 18-year-old unsaved teenager, a big tough guy, begging me to go to an evangelistic tent meeting?

"Are you serious?" This was incredulous!

"I certainly am."

"Of course, I'll go."

"Great - I'll pick you up at seven tonight!" He winked at me as he walked out.

Art proved to be a charming young man who knew how to keep a conversation going even when I was too shy to respond. I knew I could easily fall in love with this fun-loving guy, but he did not love the Lord and I was determined not to fall into that trap.

We did not go out again for several months. Then one Sunday night, he asked me to go to a Billy Graham film at a church in Winnipeg, a 40-mile drive from home. Art's brother and his girlfriend doubled with us.

The film portrayed the spiritual revival and struggles of Christians in Scotland, ending with a heart-stirring message by Billy Graham. On the way home we stopped at a Salisbury House coffee shop. Art and I sat at a table of our own and had a serious talk. He asked me to go steady with him saying he liked me and wanted to get to know me better. He especially liked my eyes!

Art realized, however, that I was having inner conflicts because he was not a Christian. He told me he was under spiritual conviction and was aware that I was praying for him. He talked of his intention to follow the Lord some day, when he was ready, but not under pressure from anyone.

My heart went out to him. How could I be so happy and so sad simultaneously? I had an opportunity to go steady with the most handsome and most popular guy in our hometown and I wanted to say yes, but the Bible clearly states that a Christian cannot be unequally yoked with an unbeliever. What could I say?

"Art, you know I have prayed so much about us. I like you, too, and I want to get to know you better. However, I love the Lord and I know you respect my convictions. I have come to the conclusion that God wants me to be your friend, but I cannot promise you more than friendship until you become a Christian, too".

Art accepted my offer of friendship. We did not date regularly but went skating occasionally. One cold, sunny February afternoon Art picked me up in his Dad's new '56 Chevy. He took me to his home, where a group of young people were having a birthday party for his sister, Annie. When Art drove me back it was still early and we had planned to spend the evening playing crokinole at my house. I had come to the realization that I was falling madly in love and getting much too attached to him. I would have to stop seeing him! How could I tell him that? Art became restless as he sensed what was coming. Our carefree spirit of the day suddenly evaporated and he left before we could get into a discussion.

The next day we happened to meet at the skating rink. Art came skating up to me, and with a shy grin he took my hand and said, "I stepped over to the Lord's side last night!"

"What did you say?" I could not believe my ears.

"I accepted the Lord last night!"

What an answer to prayer! One of his friends at the birthday party had returned later in the evening to speak to Art about his soul. Feeling depressed after leaving my house Art was ready to do some soul searching and make that all important decision to give his life over to the Lord.

Our relationship developed into deep love, both of us confident that the Lord had led us together. With His loving guidance we made wedding plans, and on Art's 21st birthday, May 1st, 1960, we were married in our country church.

After a two-day honeymoon, we settled into a tiny, one-room cabin home on the Cornelsen farm. We had an abbreviated honeymoon in order for Art to get onto the fields for spring seeding.

Although I had grown up in the country, I had not actually lived on a farm. I found it difficult at first to adjust to the frantic pace of seeding time and harvest after a fairly easy-going pace of life. The long hours Art spent on the tractor or combine seemed endless to me, and sometimes I would join him on the machinery just to spend more time with him.

The following years were busy but happy. Our firstborn, a son, Cameron Arthur, joined us a year after we were married. Three years later, Lynette Rose was born, a tiny five-and-a-half pound premature baby. Arlene Dawn arrived four years later, a healthy, bouncing girl weighing in at nine pounds and two ounces. Our family was complete, and we thanked God every night for the love and joy we had to share with each other.

Chapter Four

TROUBLE AHEAD?

My eyes blurred with unshed tears as I watched the gown-clad graduates make their way up the aisle of the church. Our daughter, Lynette, was graduating from the one-year General Bible Course at the Okanagan Bible College, Kelowna, BC. We were so proud of her. Our timid, quiet, little girl had definitely grown up into an outgoing, popular young lady, well able to hold her own. Her love for the Lord and her quiet but cheerful, sensitive nature made her a joy to have around. Judging by the hugs and tears from the dozens of people crowding around her, her friends found it as difficult as she did to say good-bye.

The college, temporarily located at a Baptist Bible camp, was nestled snugly beside a vineyard among the tall cedars and pines on the beautiful shores of the Okanagan Lake. The not-so-distant mountains were reflected in the clear, quiet waters of the lake, creating a peaceful contrast to Lynette's troubled heart. How she had learned to love this place with its enriching assortment of students from all over the country, and how she dreaded to leave it.

We watched Lynette, arm-in-arm with Mary Lynn, sauntering slowly along the dock. They had been roommates and had grown close, like sisters. In the dimming twilight, we noticed a young man joining the girls. Their growing realization of the possibility of never seeing each other again was hitting them hard. After some long, teary hugs, Lynette reluctantly joined us in the car.

"Hard to say good-bye?" I asked as we left the campus.

"Very, but I've decided to come back for second year. And Norm and I decided to work at camp together this summer, up in northern BC."

I was surprised. "When did you decide this?"

"About a month ago. The Canadian Sunday School Mission has accepted us."

"This Norm, is he kind of special?"

"You better believe it! He taught me to play the guitar and says I'm the best student he ever had. I probably was the only student he ever had, but I was the best!" Lynette giggled happily and settled back in her seat to daydream the rest of the way to my sister's house, where we spent the night.

We got up early the next morning for the long, two-day drive home. That night we stopped at a Medicine Hat motel and relaxed in a hot whirlpool before going to bed. Rising early again the next morning, Lynette dragged herself out of bed and staggered toward the bathroom.

"Too early for you, Lynsh?" her Dad asked.

"O-o-oh, yes, no-o-o, I'm so-o-o dizzy."

"Too much swimming and hot water last night," her Dad remarked.

By noon Lynette had a bad earache and she spent the rest of the trip home dozing, half-doped with Tylenol. It was wonderful having Lynette back home, but her ear infection required several trips to her doctor in the city before she got any relief from the pain and dizziness.

A month passed. Lynette's listlessness and indecision about summer employment began to irk me. One day she would plan to work in Winnipeg, the next she was planning to be a counsellor at the camp in BC.

"All right, Lynette, which will it be? If you're planning to fly to BC, we have to make reservations for your flight within one week."

"Mom, I really want to go to BC very badly, but I can't get myself to go so far away this summer. I don't feel very well yet. I get such splitting headaches. I think I'd better look for a job closer to home and share an apartment with Lori in Winnipeg."

I considered she was dismissing the camp experience too lightly and told her so.

"OK, Mom, let's do it this way. Let's pray about it. In the meantime, I'm going to look for a job and an apartment. If I find both within one week, it means God wants me to stay here; if I don't find both, I'll go to BC."

I agreed. For her to find summer employment and an apartment available within one week would take God's intervention. She picked up a city paper at the local store and pored over the want ads, circling several. The next day she asked me to go with her to Winnipeg to check them out.

Her third application was at a new Salisbury restaurant that would open shortly near Tuxedo. An immediate interview with the manager landed her the job of cashier. Lynette was jubilant! Her cousin, Lori, had heard of some university students who wanted to sublet their apartment for the summer months, and the location turned out to be excellent. There was no more talk of camps in BC

The summer of '83 proved to be one of the hottest on record. Art and Cam had taken on the construction of a huge dairy barn some 30 miles from home, and the heat tested them almost beyond endurance. We were all looking forward eagerly to the fall when Cam and Janet were expecting their baby. This anticipation helped to pull us through the long hot days and humid nights.

For Lynette the days dragged by. The novelty of her first job wore off under the scrutiny of an insensitive supervisor and some fussy, snobbish patrons. Her headaches were almost unbearable. It was with alarm that she realized she could not hear with her right ear.

"Your hearing loss is 100 per cent in your right ear and is likely permanent. It happens occasionally from a virus such as measles. Your type of virus lasts up to six or eight months. Let's just hope we can keep your hearing in the other ear!"

The ear specialist's diagnosis was not what Lynette and I expected to hear. Silently we left his office and crossed the street to the department store cafeteria where Arlene was waiting for us. We picked up our soup and beverages and carried our trays to the crowded dining area. Pushing my tray along our table, I clumsily tipped it over the edge, dumping the entire contents all over the carpet. Quickly, we managed to move unobtrusively over to another table. I decided to go without lunch that day! I was deeply disturbed by the doctor's assessment of Lynette's loss of hearing.

"If you have this virus, how will it affect your plans for college this fall?" I asked, after we were finally seated for lunch.

"You heard the doctor, Mom. He said I could go ahead. I'll just have to see a doctor out there," Lynette answered more optimistically than she felt.

A week later, Lynette boarded a plane for BC Arlene entered high school, and our harvest was well underway. After a frantic summer, life had finally taken on a normal pace again.

Chapter Five

SO MUCH TO BE THANKFUL FOR

The breeze was surprisingly warm for a mid-September evening, but the stars were no longer as bright as they had been. Occasionally, a passing cloud covered the harvest moon momentarily. I bent over to touch a blade of grass – no dew yet. The forecast was for showers. The men would have to combine late tonight to finish the last of the flax. It looked like we would be able to finish our harvest without stopping for rain.

The combines were coming down the field toward the truck to unload. I grabbed the thermos and a cinnamon roll and ran over to the truck. Cam stopped his combine and jumped off while the auger dumped the flaxseed onto the truck.

"Hi, Mom! Have you seen Janet tonight?"

"Yes, she was over earlier. Don't you recognize her cinnamon rolls? She baked them."

"Oh yeah. Come to think of it, they do taste like hers – even better than yours! Why didn't she come with you?"

"She was very tired. She helped me dig the last of the potatoes this afternoon. I think she also finished that baby blanket she was quilting. She is one ambitious girl!"

"And beautiful, even at seven months pregnant," Cam grinned as he ran back to the combine.

Art maneuvered his combine up to the truck as Cam pulled away. While his combine unloaded, he came over to the truck for a quick coffee break.

"Hi, sweetheart, good to see you! Looks like we'll finish combining tonight!

"Great! It looks like rain. If it doesn't rain too hard, we might even get our cultivating done before we leave for my niece's wedding in BC next week".

"I sure hope so. Isn't God good to us? I've been thinking tonight about our life together, Rose. God's been so good to us. Financially, we're able to make our farm payments and live a fairly comfortable life. We've been able to take some wonderful trips together. We have a healthy, normal family. Cam is happily married to a lovely Christian girl, and we're expecting our first grandchild. Lynette is a sincere Christian girl attending Bible college. Arlene has grown up and is an excellent volleyball player, also a good Christian girl. God granted you good health again after your cancer scare. You know, Rose, life just can't get any better on this side of heaven."

"You're right, Art. We have so much to be thankful for." I shouted to make myself heard above the roar of the combine motor.

As Art cheerfully moved the combine back into the windrow of flax, I thoughtfully screwed the top back onto the thermos bottle. A nagging anxiety kept pushing its way into my thoughts.

"If it can't get better, will it turn worse?" I gathered up the remains of the snack and walked slowly back to the car.

Gazing up, I caught a streak of lightening against the dark sky.

I reminded myself to call Lynette when I got home.

Arlene had just come home from a volleyball tournament when I got back and was snacking on a cinnamon bun with a glass of milk.

"So, how did the tournament go?" I asked.

"Great we actually came in second. We should have been first. We have the potential. Oh, Mom, they asked me to be the captain of our team." Arlene was beaming.

"Congratulations! I hope you have a good season. I hope I'll get to see some of your games."

Being the tallest girl on her junior varsity team, Arlene was an outstanding middle-blocker. The whole team had made quite a name for themselves the previous year, winning every tournament in southern Manitoba. This was quite an accomplishment, since they were considered a "small schools team," and the ages of the girls averaged a year younger than most players. Volleyball was Arlene's passion and she put all her energies into improving her style.

Indeed, it looked like we had a great year ahead of us. If only Lynette would be OK. . . . Her letters did not sound too encouraging but then the doctor had said it could take another month or two for the virus to die.

Chapter Six

SURGERY!

"Hi, Mom and Dad. It's super to see you!" Lynette greeted us with bear hugs even before we could get out of the car.

Art and I had driven the 1200 miles to Kelowna not only to attend my niece's wedding, but also to visit Lynette.

When we arrived on campus and caught sight of Lynette, we both had to catch our breath. Had we forgotten how beautiful she was, or had she changed? Lynette had been sick frequently that month at school, and we expected her to look less than healthy. Now, she met us with a dazzling smile, her shiny, dark hair feathered back with the longer, curly locks falling softly to her shoulders. But there was more — there was a quality about her glowing face and her large, sparkling blue eyes that seemed to belie any lurking illnesses.

Over our Chinese supper, Lynette and her friend, Kayleen, teased each other about who had the most boyfriends and how their studies suffered from too many "Mac attacks." There was little mention made of poor health except that everyone in school had had a bad flu and Lynette's bout seemed to hang on longer.

That evening Lynette came with us to Armstrong to watch the wedding rehearsal. We took a motel in Enderby for the night. I noticed Lynette took two extra-strength Tylenol capsules before she went to bed. Sleeping in the same room with her I was acutely aware of her tossing and groaning all night. I became even more alarmed when she dragged herself out of bed the next morning, dropped to the floor of the bathroom, and gagged as she threw up into the toilet. Then, pale but smiling, she dressed for the morning wedding.

The wedding was beautiful, but the reception seemed long and drawn out.

"Would you like to go back to the motel?" I had noticed Lynette was quieter than usual.

"Surely you want to stay to visit with all these relatives. You came a long way for this wedding, Mom."

"We came to see you, Lynette. Dad can stay, I'll take you back. I wouldn't mind resting myself."

"I guess I am tired, and my headache is worse," Lynette admitted.

The following night was a repetition of the first. I lay wide awake in my worry and fear. Nor was the morning scenario different.

When we took Lynette back to the campus that evening, my heart was heavy. How could she cope with her studies and manage to travel the 350 miles to Vancouver for the medical help that the doctor in Kelowna recommended? Flights were available — but what if the specialists found some serious problem? Was it fair for a young girl to have to face this by herself? These troubling thoughts were on Lynette's mind too, but she assured us she could handle it.

Together we walked up to her dormitory. Art put down her suitcase and gave her a good-bye hug.

Reverting to the pet name he had dubbed her in childhood, Art counselled, "Whatever happens, Lynshie Bird, God will help you. Be sure to phone us when you need to talk or if you need our help."

"I will. Bye Dad. Have a good trip home." She quickly brushed away a tear as she turned to me. Lynette hugged me tightly. Suddenly dropping all her defenses, she her put head on my shoulder and began to sob. I held her tightly.

"Lynette, come home with us. We'll see the doctors back home, and then you can come back again," I begged.

"No way! I'm not going to be a baby. I can handle this myself. I'm sorry I broke down. It's just that I'll miss you when you're gone again." She attempted a weak smile.

Misgivings about leaving her developed into panic as we drove away. After I cried all the way into town, Art decided to stop for coffee and talk things over. Suddenly, it became very clear what we had to do. Art called the college dean of women. She sounded relieved to hear from us. She too had been concerned and agreed we should take Lynette home for a thorough medical examination.

"Don't worry about her missing two weeks of school. All she'll miss her mid-term exams, and we'll excuse her of those."

Art then talked to Lynette by phone. She willingly agreed to be ready in half an hour!

The next two days of travel were a mad rush to get home.

Although Lynette was cheerful, we knew there was something terribly wrong with her. From Regina we called Dr. Freed in Winnipeg, making an appointment to see him late that afternoon. Upon examining her, he immediately made an appointment with a neurologist. He suspected a neuroma — a growth on her hearing nerve. Our hearts sank!

Dr. Freed warned us that the neurologist he had referred us to was a strange type of character, but that he was the best in his field. I was grateful for the warning! The doctor's blunt manner particularly grated on our emotions because of our fear of a dreaded diagnosis. He looked deep into Lynette's eyes with his examining light.

He said, "There appears to be nothing wrong neurologically. I'm going to ask you some questions, Lynette, and Mother, I don't want a peep out of you.

"Lynette," he asked abruptly, "are you pregnant?"

Lynette did not show her irritation at the question. "I'm sure I'm not," she smiled.

"Well, OK, I just had to clear that aside. Anyway, there doesn't appear to be any emergency here. You look terrific, you know. We'll put your name on the waiting list for a CAT scan. It'll take about a month."

I could not remain silent any longer. "What about her splitting headaches, loss of hearing, dizziness, vomiting? What about her classes back in BC Can't you get her a CAT scan quickly?"

"This is no emergency. Good-bye."

Lynette and I left, totally frustrated. I had to agree with the neurologist that Lynette looked gorgeous in the afternoons, but he should see her in the mornings.

Over the weekend Lynette's headaches and nausea became intense. By Tuesday I was desperate. I called different doctors, who each promised to do "something." Then I remembered the ear specialist she had seen that summer. I called and told him what the "virus" was doing and how the neurologist had brushed us off. Dr. Springer listened sympathetically and told me he would call me back within an hour or two.

That call did it! An hour later I had a collect call from the neurologist!

"Apparently something drastic has happened since you saw me," he remarked crisply. "Have Lynette see me in Emergency tomorrow at 9:00 a.m."

It was difficult to say whether we were more relieved or frightened. Would we finally get some help, or would we rather have remained ignorant of the facts? Even in our worst fears, however, we could not anticipate the nightmare that the following weeks were to bring.

From my diary:

Wednesday, October 26, 1983: Lynette, Art, and I arrived at St. Boniface Hospital but found no place to park the car and could not find the emergency entrance due to construction in that area. Who should pull up but Lynette's doctor! He recognized us and beckoned us to follow him. I stayed in the waiting room while Art took Lynette into the office. After one look into her eyes, the doctor ran for the phone. Lynette was admitted immediately and scheduled to have her CAT scan at four o'clock that afternoon.

"Stay with her. In fact, do not let her out of your sight one minute, in case of some emergency!"

Lynette was admitted into a special-care ward in the Neuroscience Wing. It was Lynette's first hospital experience, and the sight of other patients with shaved heads, some unconscious and others crying in pain, was totally shocking and left her shaking in fear. At four o'clock, Lynette, a nurse, Art, and I piled into a taxi and headed for the Health Sciences Centre for her CAT scan.

An hour later, back at the St. Boniface Hospital, we tried to settle Lynette down, but we were all too uptight. The phone rang shrilly beside Lynette's bed. The neurologist explained the results of the scan to Art by phone.

All our worst suspicions were verified. There was a tumor at the base of her brain, just above her spinal column where all the nerves emerge. The growth had attached itself to the pons and several nerves were already involved. They strongly suspected a malignancy. Surgery was imperative.

We were crushed! We told Lynette only as much as we felt she could handle at one time.

I phoned Cam and Janet to tell them the devastating news.They alerted the rest of the relatives and the church family. Prayer chains were activated. We stayed with Lynette till about 11:00 p.m. Our pastor couple, Stan and Alma Plett, as well as Elly and John Rempel [my sister and brother-in-law] and their daughter, Pam, came to visit Lynette.

Thursday, October 27, 1983:

Art and I were back at the hospital as early as possible to meet the doctor. Lynette had slept poorly and was waiting impatiently for us. We had received so many phone calls that we'd gotten away later than planned. The neurologist took Art and me into a small medical classroom. The fact that he took us to such a private room filled me with dread. He showed us the CAT scan results. They did not make much sense to me, but what the doctor said was all too clear. What my mind had tried to reject as a nightmare until now suddenly loomed as a frightful reality.

"Tumor — likely malignant — surgery — cobalt." Was it really *our* child he was talking about?

On our way back down the hall, the neurologist stopped a group of young interns and enthusiastically related the results to them.

"That CAT scan does not only show a neuroma but we suspect a posterior fossa meningioma."

One charming young intern, whom I recognized as one who had teasingly flirted with Lynette, asked with obvious concern, "You mean that lovely 19-year-old girl?"

This was my breaking point. I ran for the washroom and wept. If this diagnosis alarmed the young doctors, how were we as parents supposed to accept this? How could we face Lynette without betraying our hopeless feelings?

But face her we did. She questioned us about the interview. What lay ahead for her?

We told her that brain surgery would definitely take place within the week, but she was to have the best team of surgeons in North America, headed by Dr. Norman Miller.

"Will they shave off all my hair?" she wailed. Lynette had always taken such pride in her beautiful hair. "My best feature," she would smilingly boast.

Friday - Sunday, October 28-30, 1983

Friends began to drop in. A classmate of Lynette's, Joanne, spent a lot of time with her, frequently taking her down to the cafeteria for coffee. On Saturday she brought a saleslady from a downtown department store complete with an armful of wigs. Cam and Janet joined us for a wig party! Lynette selected one. We persuaded the nurses to wait until just before the surgery to shave Lynette's head.

More friends visited. Saturday evening when the guests numbered about 25, we all had to gather in the cafeteria. Lynette's high school sports coach stopped by to bring her a huge bouquet of flowers. He was obviously stirred by Lynette's calm acceptance of her condition.

"Her faith will see her through. She has a great Coach up there!" he declared through tears, as he embraced Art and me simultaneously. We were deeply touched by his expression of love.

One of Lynette's nurses came by when Art and I were relaxing in the lounge.

"How are you two holding up?" she asked.

"We're all right, thank-you."

"Does Lynette know the whole truth?" she asked.

"Yes, I think so," Art replied. "Whether the full impact has hit her, we don't know. She's taking it very well."

The nurse sat down on the coffee table in front of us.

"Lynette is a very brave girl. I've been very impressed by her. Last night she told me about her faith and how she trusts God to help her. She also told me about her plans to go back to school after Christmas. This must be so hard on you all. It's just totally unfair." The nurse blinked back her tears, squeezed our hands, and was gone.

Close friends of ours, a couple who had lost a young son in a tractor accident, dropped in at the hospital to visit Art and me. They caught us at a weak moment, so we went down to a quieter lounge away from Lynette, where we could weep and pray together. It seemed Lynette was holding up better than we were.

Pastor Stan Plett and his wife, Alma, as well as our Assistant Pastor Melvin Dueck and his wife, Anne, came to anoint Lynette with oil and to pray for her healing. Many churches all over Canada, U.S.A., Germany, New Zealand, and other countries joined to pray for her. Okanagan Bible College called to tell her they were having a 24-hour prayer vigil for six days. Our home church supported us with prayers, driving, food, love and concern. God's miracle of love was doing its work of upholding us. We sensed God's strength being renewed in us daily and often hourly.

"Thank you Lord, for the family of God.
Bless them!"

Monday, October 31, 1983

Halloween! Eve before the surgery.
Dozens of friends dropped in between various
pre-op tests and X-rays. At last, after
everybody left, the dreaded moment arrived. I
had promised to stay for the head shave. I did
not know how I could bear to watch it, but I
certainly could not have Lynette go through
such a heartbreaking experience alone.

When the girl came in with her razor, she
asked Lynette to sit on a chair. I lay across her
bed close by. I grabbed Lynette's shaking
hand. I knew her inner struggle when her
fingers clenched mine. I sensed the trauma she
felt as the razor began at her neck, whizzed its
way up over her crown and forward to her
bangs. Relentlessly, the razor kept going, and
the lovely hair dropped silently into a paper
bag. Soon her head was shamefully, un-
believably hairless, and her eyes, which
loomed larger than ever, filled with tears and
began to brim over. She sobbed into a facecloth
while the fuzz was being shaved off, but came
up smiling again when a toque-like pixie cap
was placed on her head.

When her dad came in a minute later and
exclaimed over her beautiful eyes, she said,
"I'm afraid I'm going to be a crybaby again."

"Come on, crawl into my arms and be my
baby," I invited. My heart ached at this painful
indignity and this was only the beginning!
Lynette moved over so I could wrap my arms

around her. For a minute we clung to each other, our tears intermingling. Then, abruptly, she sat up, her eyes twinkling as she smiled again. Art prayed with us, asking God for His peace and protection over Lynette. We prayed for a good night's sleep for her, free from anxiety. We also prayed for the team of doctors that would be working on Lynette the next day, especially for Dr. Miller who would need a steady hand and clear mind for the intricate microsurgery.

Chapter Seven

RECOVERY?

Hour after hour dragged by. Clouds of stale cigarette smoke in the crowded lounge increased the unpleasantness of the hospital surroundings as we waited for Lynette's surgery to end. We treasured the company of family and friends who came to sit with us.

Finally, after five hours, Dr. Miller, the neurosurgeon, came to inform us of the situation. As expected, they found the tumor attached to and interwoven in a very intricate part of the brain and were unable to remove much of it without seriously handicapping Lynette. He reassured us that the growth was not malignant however. For the next 48 hours she would remain in a dangerously critical condition, but after that they expected her to be fine. Lynette would require cobalt treatments and would be put on regular medication to stabilize her condition.

Art was jubilant. No malignancy! I was relieved that the operation was over, but as the surgeon talked to us I could visualize the next two years: trips to doctors, hospitals, cancer treatments, perpetual uncertainty. I felt let down. I wanted my old Lynette back. I wanted her healthy and strong, and happy, and I wanted it immediately. Lynette had plans for her future. Would she have to give them all up? I was surprised at myself. What kind of miracle had I expected? I never doubted that God's hand was in control, but somehow I had hoped for a more encouraging report. Someone suggested we go to the hospital chapel down the hall. We all joined hands, bowed our heads and poured our hearts out to God in thanksgiving, imploring Him to continue to heal Lynette.

When we were allowed into the intensive care unit, I braced myself. Art and I went in together. It was hard to believe it was actually our daughter who was attached to all those tubes and monitors. Her head was swathed in white gauze bandages, and her face was deathly pale. Her eyes were half-closed, and her tongue was slightly protruding due to a tube running down her throat.

"Lynette, Mom's here," I called softly.

She opened her eyes. What a relief! She responded! We had been warned she might not respond for several days. Another answer to prayer.

We were allowed to see her for five minutes every half-hour or so. The second time we went in we asked her if she had any pain, and she nodded her head slightly. Half an hour later she tried to speak but the tubes in her mouth prevented her. We could tell she was getting frustrated, so Art held her hand and told her to relax. Finally, with her only free finger, Lynette pointed to Art's wristwatch. Of course! She wanted to know what time it was! We were thrilled to realize that her mental capacity had not been damaged at all!

By evening everybody except Art and I had left the hospital. We were exhausted but we knew Lynette's condition was still precarious. She grabbed our hands tightly whenever we stood by her bed. She needed us desperately!

In the hall we met a fourth-floor patient who was curious as to the results of the surgery and how we were holding up.

"You know, there's a tiny chaplain's office up on the fourth floor that my family used a few weeks ago. It has an easy chair in it where you could get a rest — away from all this noise. The nurse at the desk has the key," the patient informed us.

We found a blissfully quiet, private room with a soft reclining chair. Art sneaked a mat off a stretcher in the hall and we both stretched out for about an hour.

When we checked on Lynette at eleven, she indicated that we could go home, but we knew by the way she clung to our hands that she dreaded our leaving. We promised to be back early and left.

A strange pattern of emotions began to take shape in me. As long as I was with Lynette, I was peaceful, strong and hopeful. The minute we left the hospital I would break into uncontrollable sobs. Once at home, I would attempt to be strong for Arlene's sake but every phone call would cause me to break down again. Art and I prayed together every night and then slept out of sheer exhaustion, although we always awoke early. In the morning, we would see Arlene off to school and then go to the hospital as soon as we could slip away from the phone calls.

Two days after the surgery, Lynette was able to get up and walk to the washroom with my help. She was still quite weak and getting very frustrated with her frail voice. We had thought it was the tube that kept her from talking, but now, with the tube removed, she could still only whisper.

Alarmed, I sought out Dr. Miller. He informed me that they might have damaged the nerve that controlled the voice, but that in time it should restore itself.

"And what if it doesn't?" I fretted silently.

I sat with Lynette all afternoon, reading to her, swabbing her mouth, lubricating her lips with Vaseline. She napped in between, but by late afternoon she was restless with pain and leg cramps. It seemed I could do nothing right and she could not communicate what she needed. Finally, in total defeat, she turned her head away from me and shut her eyes. I could see the tears welling out from under the closed eyelids. I had reached my limit of endurance as well and left the room.

In the lounge, a lady I had never met before, handed me a little bookmark with a story printed on it, "Footprints in the Sand." The story told of a man who dreams he is walking along a sandy beach with the Lord:

> Across the sky flashed scenes from his life. For each scene, he noticed two sets of footprints in the sand; one belonged to him, and the other to the Lord. . . . He noticed that many times along the path of his life there was

only one set of footprints. He also noticed that it happened at the very lowest and saddest times in his life. This really bothered him and he questioned the Lord, "Lord, you said that once I decided to follow you, you'd walk with me all the way. . . . I don't understand why, when I needed you most, you would leave me."

The Lord replied, "My precious, precious child, I love you and I would never leave you. During your times of trial and suffering, when you see only one set of footprints, it was then that I carried you."
- Author Unknown

Encouraged, I went back to share this story with Lynette. I saw she had just received two cards in the mail. They were both identical to the one in my hand! Lynette smiled at me and whispered, "You think God is trying to tell me something?"

The day had been a rough one, and we both needed just such an encouragement.

We were learning to lean on Jesus and to depend on promises like Isaiah 40:29-30:

He gives power to the tired and worn-out and strength to the weak. Even the youths shall be exhausted and the young men will all give up. But they that wait upon the Lord shall renew their strength. They shall mount up with wings as eagles. They shall run and not be weary, they shall walk and not faint.

God's mercies are new every morning and we were given the opportunity to prove them! The following months were most difficult but enriching. Together we learned to renew our depleted resources of strength by asking God to carry us again and again.

Not only was Lynette's voice affected by the surgery, but her swallowing was inhibited as well. Her balance was unstable and at first she required assistance in walking. Much to my dismay, she was discharged from the hospital exactly one week after surgery. Once home she realized that she was not quite as strong as she had led the doctors to believe, but, somehow we managed.

A month went by, during which Lynette had appointments with radiologists at the Cancer Clinic in Winnipeg Health Sciences Center. In preparation for cobalt treatments, she had to go for molding of her plastic head mask. This would protect her healthy cells from exposure to the deadly radioactivity. She was put on a cortisone medication, Decadron, to shrink the swelling around the tumor. Cimetidine protected the stomach lining from the cortisone. It took weeks before Lynette could sleep through the night — another side effect of her medication. During this convalescent period, many friends stopped by to show their love and concern. I would check up on Lynette three or four times a night; often, I just sat and talked with her or massaged her back and legs. At other times, I would lie down beside her to keep her company through those long, dark hours. There were times I would simply pray Lynette through her most painful hours. Time did eventually pass, however, and her strength slowly returned.

In the midst of those dark, fall days, a bright spot suddenly appeared. In the wee hours of Sunday, November 20, little Curtis Allen was born to Cam and Janet.

"Let's go see him," Lynette whispered eagerly.

"Are you up to it?" I asked, surprised. Art and I had planned to drive to the Winnipeg hospital to visit our first grandchild, but we had not expected to take the girls.

"Of course, she can go, Mom. I'm coming, too," Arlene joined in.

The young aunties and grandpa were delighted to see the baby through the nursery window, but grandma had the heady pleasure of actually holding the soft, warm treasure in her arms.

"Isn't he cute as a button?" grinned Janet, a proud new mother.

"Cute as his mother. He's sensational! I have to admit that he's the most beautiful baby I've ever seen!" It was really true — perhaps I was slightly biased but this child had the loveliest head of thick, dark hair I had ever seen. Cam and Janet were both fair-haired.

"Well, what could you expect from two people like Janet and me?" the glowing father boasted.

"Of course, of course! But really, let's thank God everything's all right here!"

They agreed.

Curtis was going to be our sunshine in a world that seemed to have turned so dark for us.

On November 28, Lynette had her first cobalt treatment. Her hair had been coming in beautifully, all dark and shiny. When dressed up, with make-up and earrings, she looked perfectly chic. Her high cheek bones and large eyes gave her a sophisticated appearance. The cobalt, aimed at the tumor from a spot behind each ear, caused the hair to fall out in those areas. Nevertheless, Lynette's good spirits were helping us all to regard her condition more optimistically.

Each day for thirty days, church friends took turns driving Lynette and me to Winnipeg for her daily treatments. After the last treatment, an elderly radiologist looked at her CAT Scan and muttered, "I'd hoped we'd see more improvement." Despite the depressing news, we decided to celebrate by having lunch at a chicken and rib restaurant.

> Thou wilt keep him in perfect peace whose mind is stayed on thee because he trusteth in thee. Isaiah 26:3

Chapter Eight

RESPITE

"Come on, say you'll go — the change will do you good."

We were aware of the plans that were in the making by a group of Rosenort couples. In fact, a year earlier, Art had organized the same group of people to go to Texas for a week of construction work at the Rio Grande Bible Institute (RGBI). The subsequent week was spent at a holiday resort in southern Mexico. I knew how much Art longed to go again, but I hesitated. How could I leave Lynette just a week after her final cobalt treatment? Was it not totally irresponsible of me to leave her for over two weeks?

The doctor's checkup proved Lynette was making good progress, and he could see no reason for Art and me to stay home. One of Lynette's Bible college friends offered to fly out from BC to stay with the girls. After much prayer, we received peace about leaving and packed up.

The work week at the RGBI campus involved brick laying and roof building on a boys' dormitory. The men worked hard while their wives shopped, visited, and became acquainted with the campus staff and students.

A killing frost had destroyed the orange and grapefruit crops in the area. The palm trees that had once ennobled the landscape with their majestic height, were now hanging their heads, with branches brown and limp. The people were friendly and cheerful, however, and we thoroughly enjoyed our "working holiday." Our group was planning to travel into Mexico during the second week.

"There's a very picturesque train ride from Chihuahua City going west through the mountains to Las Moches on the coast. Shall we go?" Art asked me one night after work.

"Is the rest of the group going?" I would have preferred to fly home directly, but I knew Art would be disappointed.

The train ride was everything and more than I had expected. We had been told it would take all day to get to the coast, but nobody had told us that half the time would be spent making stops! However, the stops were far from boring. Pedlars, Indian men, women, and children would hop aboard the train in hordes, selling their crafts of excellent workmanship. We were able to communicate with the few Spanish words we knew, haggling over a woven rug, reed basket, or even the fruit they brought with them. They would offer us "cafe" from filthy, battered antifreeze cans. Babies with bare bottoms and runny noses would hang on to their heavily dressed mothers as they made their way back and forth, showing off intricately embroidered tea cloths.

Before we left Chihuahua City, a fellow tourist, obviously Canadian by his heavy French accent, advised us of a delightful stopover in the mountains, about three hours east of the coast.

"In fact, if you stay there for a few days, you'll see more than if you go to the coast," he told us.

After seven hours of stops and starts, endless rounds of card games and a foray into a dining car of dubious merit, we were more than ready to stay at the Catholic mission hotel that the French-Canadian had raved about.

When the train arrived at our destination we were dismayed to find rain coming down in torrents. Through the heavy downpour we could barely make out the sign on the station platform, 'Bahuichivo Estacion.' A battered, old bus bearing the name "Hotel Mision" stood in readiness. Grabbing our suitcases, we scrambled off the train, across the tracks and into the waiting vehicle. Long after it was full, people kept crowding into the old bus.

We were pleased with the front seats we had secured until our journey began. At that point we would been just as happy not to see the operation of the bus. A willing passenger was recruited to wipe off the fogged-up windows; however, the real problem was the non-operative windshield wiper. Nonetheless, the blinding rain and fading daylight did nothing to impede our speed of travel. Singing merrily at the top of his voice, the jovial bus driver swished and swerved his swaying vehicle through rain-filled potholes up the side of the mountain, down the steep road back into the valley, and across the narrow bridges. The bus stopped only now and then to release a few passengers or pick up a new, soggy traveller. We were amazed when the sputtering bus successfully negotiated the next steep mountain. In the deepening dusk, we could just make out the sheer drop of the cliff to our left. I closed my eyes to shut out the impending dangers.

After an hour of this nerve-racking progress, faint light finally glimmered out of the darkness ahead. We came to an abrupt stop in front of a quaint Spanish-Catholic Mission Hotel. It was dark by now and the lobby of the inn was dimly lit by oil lamps. We seemed to be the only tourists staying there, but this did not surprise us. Surely we had arrived at the end of the earth! Would I ever see my home again?

Our assigned rooms were attractively Mexican in style and decor, clean and spacious with private baths, although the hot water ran cold. Heating was offered by a small wood-stove sitting on a low platform in one corner, with a can of diesel fuel standing close by. Our group of eight had arrived too late for the inn's evening meal, so we improvised by eating the last of our crackers and cheese. Somebody discovered half a bag of chocolate cookies in his suitcase and another came up with a couple of cans of cola. We shared our feast in the romantically soft light of the flickering lamp. Underneath our merriment ran an undercurrent of uneasiness, however. The rains were still coming down as heavily as three hours ago, and there was no sign of their slackening off. Even the local people were not used to this. We wondered about mountain road washouts. What had we gotten ourselves into? Would there by any way out of here tomorrow?

"Have you noticed there are no phones?" Art asked me. "The closest one is back at the train station."

"What if we're stuck here for a week or month. Nobody at home knows where we are," I worried. "What if something happens at home . . . ?"

"I know, I thought of that too. Maybe it wasn't a good idea to come here, after all. We'll just take the first bus out of here in the morning. It's a good thing God knows where we are! Why don't we have a prayer meeting right here?" Art suggested.

Everybody agreed. There, in the strange hotel room, eight persons took turns thanking the Heavenly Father for His protection for continued safety. We begged for the rains to stop and asked for God's care of our families at home. Although our friendships had been warm thus far, the day's experience drew us closer with a love that comes only through facing dangers together.

I kept reminding myself that our girls back home were also in God's hands. "Remember, God can take better care of them than I can," I told myself for the thousandth time.

I must have finally fallen asleep, for when I awoke sunlight was streaming through the window and all I could hear was a crowing rooster. No rain! Art had left quietly to explore the apple-treed courtyard. The fire had died out and the room was cold. The hot water faucets were still running cold, so I scrapped the idea of a bath. I dressed hurriedly and joined the rest of our shivering but grinning gang. After a good breakfast of Mexican pancakes, refried beans, pepper sauce, and strong black coffee, we were all eager to explore our surroundings.

It was unbelievable how the bright morning sun could transform the world! Advertised as the "most remote mountain tourist resort in the world" our surroundings also proved themselves among the most picturesque! The mission station comprised of our charming 28-room hotel, a beautiful Catholic church, a small village with shops, and a grocery store. Its primary focus, however, was the orphanage, adjacent to the hotel. When touring the girls' home, our hearts were touched when we saw them delightfully dressed in brightly colored skirts and blouses but huddling to keep warm under blankets on the dirt floor. They were working at handicrafts, excellently made, which they sold in their curio shop to support the home.

Although there were interesting side tours to view the Urique Grand Canyon, a mesa lumber mill, an old mining area, Indian caves, and giant waterfalls, we were determined to catch the first bus to the train station. The bus ride out was no less wild than the journey in, but we were too fascinated by the scenery to notice. There were pueblos, dilapidated shacks, and tiny red mud-brick houses, cradled in valleys dotted with apple and peach orchards and surrounded by the mountains of the Tarahumara Sierra. Along the mountain road, grotesque rock formations and swollen streams completed the exotic appeal of the 35-minute ride.

The train ride back was a mirror image of the previous day's trek. We noticed that at certain inclines the passenger cars would jerk, as if the engine were faltering. We kept on moving but was it just my imagination that we were slowing down?

"Quit worrying, Rose. You're paranoid! Relax and enjoy yourself. You'll probably never see scenery like this again."

"You've got that right! Just take me home!" I wailed miserably. I knew I was spoiling everyone's pleasure, but oh, how I longed to get back to my girls!

The train inched its way along. Gradually we left the mountains behind, but the train was definitely losing speed. Our car was getting cold. Like the orphan girls we had seen that morning, we huddled under a serape I had wrangled from an Indian pedlar. The train jerked and shuddered to a grinding halt. It was almost midnight and we were stuck somewhere on the northern plains of Mexico, just east of Cuauhtémoc.

The dark-mustached conductor sauntered through the train announcing something in Spanish. Seeing us tourists he said, "No worry, we feex train. Maybe one hour, maybe two. Soon go."

"Muchos gracias!" Art thanked him.

My heart sank when we began reversing our tracks to return the several miles to the Cuauhtémoc station. I peered out of the train window — snow on the ground! Shivering in the cold, we grabbed shirts, sweaters, slacks and longjohns from our suitcases and pulled them on in an attempt to warm up. We huddled closer together.

Dick, our music lover and choir director at our church, began to sing, and we all joined in.

"O Lord my God, when I in awesome wonder, consider all the worlds Thy hands have made . . . How great Thou art!"

As we sang one hymn of praise after another, my heart calmed down, and I became aware of the wonderful peace and love that God was offering to me. I thanked God my Father for this opportunity to experience His care in this outlandish place with these precious Christian friends. I squeezed Art's hand and he whispered, "Love you!"

It was a tired, dishevelled octet that staggered into Chihuahua City's El Presidente Hotel at 2:00 a.m., but a group ever so thankful to be back in more civilized surroundings once again. Tomorrow we would be homeward bound!

A few days later when we arrived home we found the girls overjoyed to the point of tears. Although they had insisted on the phone that they were managing all right, they had had difficulties with the snow blocked driveway, as well as Lynette's increasing headaches. We were safe at home now, however, and everybody was content.

Almost. Were our plans for the next trip sheer folly?

Chapter Nine

FURTHER REPRIEVE

"Please, Dad, please! Take us along this time. I've never been to California. I can miss a week of school, no problem! Please, Dad. Don't leave us alone again," begged Arlene. "After all, Lynette needs a change of scenery!" That argument was a clincher as she well knew.

As provincial chairman of the relief organization, Mennonite Disaster Service, Art was required to attend the annual convention being held in Los Angeles. We had reserved air flight tickets for a departure three days after returning from our Mexican trip. Our friends, Melvin and Anne Dueck, would be accompanying us, and I had been looking forward to this trip more than the previous one. However, I dreaded leaving the girls again. Moreover, I knew how my anxieties could distress others around me.

"Hey, that's an answer!" I chimed in on Arlene's pleas. "It's a great idea but I'm not sure Lynette is up to it."

"Who, me? Not up to lying in the sun? There's nothing in this world I do better than that," retorted Lynette.

"It's going to cost a pretty penny, but it might be worth the peace of mind," Art said, winking at me. "If we can get some reasonably priced tickets, we'll take you!"

"Yippee, I can miss those biology tests. Won't the kids be jealous of my mid-winter suntan! I can hardly wait. Mom, we have to go shopping, I need a new swim suit."

"Oh, wow, what did I get myself into now?" I wondered half aloud.

A nearby travel agency had bought up a large number of sale seats and was eager to sell us the two extra tickets for the girls. The seats were on another airline so Art decided to fly with Lynette, while Arlene and I took the earlier flight.

We spent the first two days at the convention and the next two days at Knotts Berry Farm and Disneyland. Melvin and Anne had brought their 10-year-old son, Jodi, along with them, and it was hard to tell whether he or Melvin was more excited about the rides.

The trip was special to all of us, because Melvin also had been sick for many years. He had undergone at least a dozen major surgeries, including an ileostomy, and had recovered from a point near death time and time again, only to have some new ailment assail him. Eventually, his ill health forced him to give up the full-time pastorate of our church, although we were still blessed with his part-time ministry as assistant pastor.

Melvin "Job" Dueck became our affectionate nickname for our dear friend, so familiar with pain and hardship. He accepted it with the graciousness so integral to his character. Melvin attracted many people into his hospital room because of his cheerful attitude. We spent many hours with Anne and him during some of his greatest battles, but we always came away feeling uplifted. Trying to forget his own pain, he would invariably center his attention on us and our problems. He and Anne were the perfect companions for our family on this trip.

When we moved from Anaheim to Palm Springs, Lynette and Arlene were in their glory. We exchanged the rain and cool temperatures of Los Angeles for warm sunshine and swimming pools. Lounging on the sun deck, I could not help but reflect on the goodness of God.

We had come through some extremely difficult months, but God had always been there to help us. He had taken Art and me all the way to Mexico and back without incident other than my impatience and anxieties. He had also kept our girls safe at home. And now He had made it possible for us all to come out, in the midst of winter, to the land of summer! I could feel the warm breeze that was waving the palm branches high above me. Lynette's thoughts must have been running along the same vein.

"Is this for real, Mom? I can't believe I'm here. The sun feels so-o-o good!" she sighed contentedly.

"Yeah. Hey, Lynette — look at that hunk on the diving board. I think I'll go swimming!" Arlene exclaimed. She was gone with a splash, Jodi right behind her.

"Want a sip?" Art handed me a cool drink.

"Where are Melvin and Anne?" I asked.

"Gone for a walk. They've been gone for an hour."

The day went by quickly and I began to make plans for the next day. It would be Lynette's 20th birthday, and we had to do something to make it extra special for her. She woke up the next morning with a headache.

"Happy birthday, Lynette!"

"Thanks! It's supposed to be a great day, isn't it?" she responded not too enthusiastically.

"Maybe you'd better stay out of the hot sun today," I suggested.

"And miss suntanning? That's what I came here for," she retorted.

"Just take it easy, OK?"

She shrugged her shoulders. She was unhappy but I was determined to cheer her up. The girls went out to the poolside again, but it wasn't long before Lynette went up to her room and lay down. She did not care to go shopping with us, so Arlene stayed with her.

We had been exploring the shops for a while and I had just ordered a corsage of red and white mums for Lynette, when Jodi came tearing around the corner.

"Guess what, I saw a movie star!" he said excitedly.

"Oh sure," I said. Jodi was always seeing movie stars.

"Honest. I saw this lady and I asked Dad if she was a movie star and Dad said, "Yes, I think so," so I went up to her and asked her if she was Elizabeth Taylor and she smiled and said yes and I asked her for her autograph and she signed this paper. See?" Jodi was breathless with excitement.

"Fantastic! And we had to miss all the fun, eh? You'll really have the best souvenir to show your friends back home," I said.

"Hey, yeah, I think I'll go shopping with you and your dad next time Jodi," Art exclaimed.

That evening we all went out for supper, making Lynette our honored guest. She was smiling bravely and valiantly attempted to eat her meal. She was pretty with the corsage pinned onto her new pink "California" sweat shirt. She smiled obediently for the camera, although she hated to be photographed her chubby face was swollen as a side effect of her medication.

"I look like a chipmunk," she would lament.

Walking back to the motel, Anne fell into step beside Lynette. I could hear their conversation.

"How are you enjoying the holiday, Lynette?" she asked.

"It's OK, but I'm getting tired. It's good to see Jodi so excited. He's really lucky to have actually seen a movie star!"

"It's really something, isn't it?" Anne replied.

"Yeah, really, but I've been thinking about that. You know, it's great to see movie stars, but I'm looking forward to seeing the really great men like Moses, Abraham, Joseph. I think that's exciting and I'll be going to meet them soon."

Later, in our room, we had a birthday cake with candles, but Lynette's interest in her birthday was long gone. She thanked us for our efforts and went to bed.

Art and I closed the glass doors behind us and gazed out into the cool night as we stood on the balcony. We stood silently, with his arms wrapped around me. As was so often the case, we were thinking the same thing.

"How long can this go on?" Art asked at last.

"I don't know. Maybe I shouldn't have made such a big deal of her birthday. She obviously tried to enjoy it only for our sakes," I said sadly.

"If we hadn't celebrated, she'd have been disappointed. No, I'm glad we did this, but I think it's time to go home. Melvin's not feeling well, either," Art replied.

"I know, that's why Melvin and Anne go on such long walks. Anne says that Melvin has sharp pains in the liver area and that walking relieves it somewhat. Why does God let His most faithful people suffer so much?" I wondered.

"I'm sure they'll get their rewards for it someday, but in the meantime I think it makes other people wonder where they get their strength from to face these hard times. Maybe it will draw others to God as a result. Let's pray for Melvin and Lynette right now." Art pulled me closer.

We prayed.

Chapter Ten

RELAPSE

"The brain scan shows it is all gone," pronounced the radiologist.

Lynette smiled and said, "That's good."

The doctor gave us a puzzled look as we left his office.

Lynette and I walked quietly to the hospital cafeteria, where we had arranged to meet Art.

"Exactly what did the doctor say?" Lynette asked me, finally.

I laughed a little. "I'm not sure! He said, 'it's all gone,' I think."

"I don't believe it. I just don't believe it!" was all Lynette could say.

It was too much to take in. Did this mean the nightmare was all over? Why wasn't the doctor more excited about the good news? Was the tumor indeed gone? Art was exuberant when we told him, but Lynette simply could not believe her problems were over.

I could not either. The radiologist's statement bothered me; something did not add up. The next day I contacted him by phone.

"Doctor, did you say Lynette's brain tumor is all gone?" I asked.

There was silence at the other end for several seconds before I heard what I expected.

"No, I didn't say that. I said the *swelling* is all gone."

Lynette was not even surprised when I told her of our misinterpretation of the doctor's report.

The medication, Decadron, which Lynette had been taking to reduce the swelling of the tumor, was producing unpleasant side effects, such as weight gain, sleeplessness, a puffy face, facial hair growth, interrupted menstrual cycle, and a slightly drugged feeling. As the amounts she took were gradually reduced her old symptoms reappeared: headaches and nausea. The doctors continually reassured us that they were simply the normal symptoms of withdrawal. Nevertheless, in April, just as Lynette was down to one tablet per day, she began to get weaker and her speech slurred slightly.

Every day for almost two weeks, I tried to reach one of our neurologists. Lynette's condition was obviously deteriorating. As the right side of her face was getting more paralyzed and her smile became increasingly crooked.

To cheer things up I decided to barbecue some steaks one day. The weather was extremely mild for the time of year. We had just started eating when Lynette let out a cry.

"I just can't take it anymore. I keep biting my cheek. I can't even chew food!" She wept in frustration.

"That does it. We've got to get help."

Finally, after some desperate phone calls, I managed to get an appointment once again with the neurologist. We went through the same fearful ordeal of examinations and tests that we had had half a year ago. The neurologist ordered another brain scan, studied it and turned Lynette over to Dr. Miller, the neurosurgeon. Dr. Miller increased her medication again but told Lynette there was no remedy other than another surgery to remove the tumor completely.

"But you told us in November you didn't have equipment to do this microsurgery. Will we have to go somewhere else?"

"Oh, didn't I tell you? Someone donated $90,000 worth of equipment in February, exactly what we need for Lynette's type of tumor. I'm confident that we can be successful this time."

This report was encouraging. The doctor tentatively slated the surgery for a month later and told Lynette she could go home until she was notified.

The next morning, was a Saturday, and Arlene came to wake me early.

"Mom, come quickly. Lynette is crying!"

I rushed up the stairs taking two steps at a time. I found Lynette, groaning in pain with a headache and nausea. I handed her the Decadron, Tylenol, and a glass of water. She swallowed the medication, sat back a minute and then grabbed the bucket that I was holding in readiness, knowing what to expect.

She was completely exhausted after her retching.

"Mom, I'm so scared! My whole left side is numb. I can hardly feel my leg at all!"

What could we do? After a few minutes, she tried to take the medication again and it stayed down. She slept a while. She refused any suggestion of seeing the doctor. However, by Sunday morning, after a long sleepless night, she agreed to let us call Dr. Miller. He had given us his home number in case of emergency.

Dr. Miller was very sympathetic and urged us to admit her into the Health Sciences Centre immediately. Poor Lynette! She was shaking with fear.

Dr. Miller explained the gravity of the situation to us. He had looked at Lynette's latest CAT Scan. The tumor was actually growing and bulging out of the cavity where the bone at the back of her skull had been removed in the previous operation. The growth was very entangled around all the vital nerves. Left alone, it would mean certain death within a year. Surgery was also risky, with a 50-50 chance of survival. If she survived, there was an even higher risk that she would spend the rest of her life in a wheelchair, possibly a paraplegic. Moreover, if her swallowing nerve was damaged again she might also have to be tube-fed for the rest of her life. What alarming prospects!

"But that's not living!" I blurted out. "Why torture her with surgery if the risk is so great?"

"Without surgery there is no hope. With surgery there is some hope. Would you deny her that?" The doctor answered quietly. "Besides, she's old enough to make her own decision."

Of course! The decision was Lynette's. There was never a question in her mind as to what she had to do. Certainly she dreaded the ordeal, and feared the worst prospects but she had to grab whatever dim hope was offered. She wanted so much to live, and to live a normal life.

We felt pushed against a wall with only darkness around and yet all was not dark. We were forced to look up, where we found light. Although we would despair whenever we looked at the situation, putting our trust in Jesus and asking Him to carry us all through would put the smile back on our faces. Once again we received the assurance that God was fully in control. He would not allow anything to happen that was not in His will, and He promised to see us through. We leaned on the Lord who loved us, and we loved Him too.

When Art and I arrived at the hospital the day before Lynette's surgery, we found her trembling in bed. Her shaven head was swathed in bandages: just after having grown long enough to style, her lovely hair was all shorn off again. Lynette had talked the doctors into letting her keep the front hair, however, so her bangs peeked out from under the bandages.

"What happened?" I asked in alarm. I noticed a tube attached to her head.

"They drilled a hole in my head this morning," she said shakily. "They have to drain off some spinal fluid from the brain to relieve the pressure before the surgery. I was hoping they'd put me to sleep for it but they only gave me a local anesthetic. I could actually hear the drill boring into my skull. Oh, Mom, I was so petrified, I was shaking uncontrollably. But Dr. Miller was so kind! He sat down beside me and held my hand. He asked another doctor to finish the job while he just held me!"

Tears filled my eyes as I pictured the busy neurosurgeon caring enough for a young patient's emotional trauma to comfort her like that.

That afternoon a student choral group from Lynette's former college arrived at the hospital to sing for her. We gathered in the lounge, and Lynette was allowed 15 minutes away from her room. While they sang, several of the girls broke down and cried. I struggled too, thinking of what might have been. Why couldn't Lynette be healthy and hearty, without a care in the world like this bunch of kids? What about all her plans for the future?

Other friends dropped in to see her. Many of her high school classmates came, and they all left in tears. Lynette's attempt to smile was heartbreaking to everybody.

Lynette had been shivering with a bad case of nerves all day. That evening after everybody left, Art and I sat down beside her bed. I held her hand and carefully broached a subject that had been on my mind all day.

"Lynette, since this is on all our minds anyway, why don't we talk about it? Wouldn't you feel better to talk about dying?"

Her eyes filled with unshed tears, "Yes, I'd like that. Actually, I've thought about it, and I think dying might not be so bad. I'd rather die than go through this surgery! If I die, please don't have a sad funeral. I want it to be victorious. If only one person should come to know the Lord because of what I have experienced, it will have been worth it."

Tears flowed freely that evening. We read the Bible together, held hands and prayed. Our hearts were at peace to know that, living or dying, Lynette was safe in God's keeping. It was very difficult to leave her for the night, but we desperately needed some rest to cope with the anxieties of the morrow. The date was May 1, Art's 45th birthday and our 24th wedding anniversary. We had hardly noticed!

Chapter Eleven

SURGERY #2

After a fitful, short night at home, Art and I left early for the hospital. It was a very quiet ride, each of us wondering what the day would hold. How could we live through such another traumatic day? We arrived before Lynette was taken down and found her shaking like a leaf again. I took her hand and prayed for peace, but the orderlies interrupted us. The stretcher had come for her ride down. She was so afraid! All I could pray was, "Lord, help her." We went with her on the elevator to the seventh floor, where she was immediately taken from us. I wondered if I'd ever see her alive again.

Our long vigil had begun. We went to investigate the Operating Room waiting area. We were not familiar with the Health Sciences Centre where Lynette was having this operation. We found a very comfortable lounge, where several families had sacked out for the past two nights. We could not sit still, so we went downstairs for coffee. When we came back up, friends and family members began to arrive to keep us company in our vigil. Cam and Janet were with us most of the time and were a great comfort. Arlene tried to function normally at school, but soon she too showed up at the hospital. Back home many friends were fasting and praying throughout the day, and we were very much aware of God's sustaining hand. I was surprised at my calmness. Somehow I knew this would not be our most difficult day — tomorrow would be infinitely harder. Today we had friends around us, would we be alone on the morrow?

By 3:30 p.m. we began to inquire about Lynette. The doctor had warned of a lengthy operation, but the suggested 8-9 hours had already elapsed. By 6:00 and 7:00 p.m. there was still no news. At 8:00 p.m. they told us it could possibly go until 10:30 or 11:00 p.m. Our alarm increased.

Had something gone wrong? Some of us decided to go to the chapel for special prayer. We all prayed, wept, and interceded some more. Suddenly, with tears streaming down his face, Cam raised his hands and exclaimed, "The Holy Spirit is here and is telling me that everything is going to be all right." Coming from Cam, I was confident that this was no emotional high. How good of God to have this reassurance come through Cam, who had been searching for answers so long. We thanked God and left the chapel with peaceful hearts.

Upon exiting the elevator on the seventh floor, we ran into Dr. Miller, who was looking for us. He looked exhausted, but he was beaming with a grin from ear to ear!

"Lynette's doing fine. We got all of the tumor out, roots and all," were his first words. He went on to tell us that he had never seen a growth so badly entangled among all the nerves. To get to the roots he had to shave slightly into the cerebellum. This would affect her balance, swallowing, breathing and heartbeat, he informed us. He was sure she'd eventually walk again, perhaps even get her hearing back. He wasn't sure about her facial paralysis.

"But," he warned, "it's a miracle she has survived thus far and the next 48-72 hours are going to be very, very critical! She'll probably be in the hospital here for three to four weeks and then she'll need about three months in the Rehabilitation Hospital to learn to walk."

Dr. Miller had been operating on Lynette for 13 hours and he looked haggard.

"You must be exhausted, Doctor," I remarked.

His smile returned and he admitted, "A little."

He told us that the surgery would have been impossible without the new ultrasound suction equipment. Lynette was only the fourth patient he had used it with.

"Dr. Miller, the ultra sound equipment, and God," I mused.

We returned to the rest of the family members, who were impatiently watching from a distance. We related the miraculous news. The "praise God's," hugs and kisses, tears and laughs intermingled. Others began to inquire what had happened, and we were able to tell of God's wonderful workings.

We were allowed to see Lynette in the ICU. She was fully awake and immediately squeezed our hands. She had tubes protruding from her nose, mouth, arms, and bladder and had monitors for everything, but she looked great to us. She held our hands very tightly trying to keep us close to her, but because the nurse had to check her constantly, we could only stay a few minutes at a time. Her eyes crossed badly when she tried to focus on us, so we encouraged her to shut them until she got stronger.

That night my sister Eva, and her husband, Henry, arrived to stay at the hospital with us.

Lynette had a fairly good night, sleeping a lot. It could have been a coincidence that her night nurse was a Christian who had attended a Bible college in BC and was instantly drawn to Lynette, but I am convinced it was God who placed her there. Later on she visited Lynette in the neuro ward as well as in the Rehab.

That morning while I was sitting with Lynette, her new day nurse asked me to keep an eye on the monitor while she went for coffee. I began to panic when the heartbeat did not register on the monitor and the choppy line dwindled down to a straight line. Just then the nurse returned. Quietly but very quickly she checked Lynette's vital signs manually and disconnected the monitor.

"Sorry for the scare," she apologized, "the machine isn't working properly. . . . Her vital signs are excellent."

With further optimism the nurse advised that Lynette was being moved down to the ward on 2D. This frightened me. It was supposed to be good news, but I didn't think Lynette had rallied enough to be transferred out of intensive care yet. What about Dr. Miller's pronouncement that the first 48 hours would be extremely critical? Only 14 hours had elapsed so far.

By noon Lynette had been moved down. She was frightened when the oxygen was removed and she had to breathe on her own. Within an hour, it was obvious that she couldn't hold her own. Janet and I took turns making her cough and spit up. She was unable to swallow and kept choking on her own saliva as well as the postsurgical congestion. The doctors began to plan an emergency tracheotomy, but they had difficulty locating the right personnel to do it. When Lynette's breathing became even more labored, I panicked. Leaving Janet with Lynette, I ran to the lounge where Cam and Art were pacing the floor.

"She can't make it — she can't make it!" I cried.

Alarmed, Art strode over to the nurses' desk where the resident doctor was calmly reading. "What's happening with Lynette? Why isn't something being done to relieve her breathing?" Art demanded.

Another doctor arrived to explain in great detail what they had decided to do.

My patience finally ran out and I exploded. "Just go and do it — she's going to die."

He ran!

Soon after, Lynette passed out when they inserted a tube down her nose and throat. The next day, unable to speak aloud, she scribbled weakly, "Yesterday I wanted to die." She also wrote that if Janet hadn't been there, she would have died.

I believed Lynette. Janet had truly kept Lynette going, encouraging her and helping her sit up when her breathing became unbearably labored. I was disappointed with myself for panicking. I was angry with the hospital staff and I was angry that Lynette had to suffer setback after setback. My heart broke to see Lynette struggling against such overwhelming odds. However, I was humbly grateful to Janet who, because of her deep attachment to her sister-in-law and despite her dislike of hospitals, frantically helped fight for Lynette's life.

O Lord, bless Janet. Thank-you, I breathed quietly.

The next day the resident doctor came over to Lynette and asked her why her eye was taped shut. I was furious! Sitting behind the nurses' station throughout the crisis the previous day, yet he still had not read Lynette's chart. He became very interested when I went into detail as to all she had come through and how pleased Dr. Miller was with her recovery. As soon as Dr. Miller came in to check on Lynette, the resident doctor, as well as all the ward nurses, surrounded her bed to hear what the specialist would say. When he repeated, "Super, just super!" they grinned as if receiving personal commendation for her condition.

Privately Dr. Miller confided to Art, "I'm surprised she survived that choking spell. Her throat is paralyzed, but she looks favorable now."

After the incident, the entire staff seemed to take a more personal interest in Lynette. It continued to anger me, however, when personnel came on duty without reading her charts. How could they possibly give her proper care and attention without knowing her medical history? Nevertheless, once made aware of Lynette's situation, the staff was terrific. Her attendants were very perceptive of her needs and often went out of their way to improve her comforts.

Physical therapy began two days after surgery by sitting up for one hour. The next day Lynette stood on her feet for a few seconds. Very slowly, she began to gain strength. On the tenth day she was taken to the physiotherapy gym, where she was given a walker. On her first try she walked the length of the gym. Two days later when she walked all the way back to her room, the nursing staff lined the hall, cheering and clapping.

At about this time she developed pneumonia. It was suspected she had swallowed food down her windpipe. Friends dropped in to cheer her up and the wall by her bed was covered with cards. Bouquets of flowers covered the tables and nightstands.

In spite of Lynette's ups and downs, Dr. Miller was still optimistic and made plans to move her to the Rehab. Surely this meant progress!

On May 23, exactly three weeks after surgery, I went to Lynette's room and found her bed stripped. A strange emotion ran through my being. Although I was expecting Lynette to be moved, I was unprepared to find her bed empty. Even her cards and clothes were gone. The nurses cheerfully informed me that I'd find her at the Rehab.

Art and I had scouted around earlier and found the underground passage to the hospital, so now I set off for the Rehab via the tunnel. Up on the fifth floor, I located the room but her bed was surrounded by a curtain. The Rehab doctor was interviewing and examining her. After an hour the doctor came out, and I found Lynette in tears.

"I don't like this one little bit," she wept. "I want to go back to the other hospital — I don't like these nurses, and this doctor wants to operate again."

"You must be kidding. Operate on what?"

"My eye and my throat." Her eye was still weak and covered with a patch. Her swallowing had not improved either, and she had problems with her eating.

"Come on, Lynette. There will be no surgery unless we okay it, I promise that won't be for a long, long time, if ever. It takes time to heal up from the last one. Be patient."

"Be patient, be patient, be patient." Lynette exploded. "I'm tired of feeling like this, and you always say, 'be patient'."

"I know, I'm sorry, but it's all we can do right now. You won't have time to be bored here. Now you can start really getting well."

"Will I have to be in here for three months like Dr. Miller said?"

"I doubt it. Dr. Miller says he's making no more predictions because you've been making a liar out of him. If he says three months, it will probably be only two."

"Whoopee," muttered Lynette, unimpressed.

When her supper was brought in — rice custard and mashed potatoes — I asked for a suction machine, just in case.

"What for?" asked her nurse, innocently.

"Oh boy, here we go again," I thought to myself.

I explained about Lynette's paralyzed throat and the possibilities of choking. She confessed she was a "floater" nurse and knew nothing about Lynette's case. I felt my temper rising.

The staff began a frantic search for a suction machine. The only one in the centre was a stationary one on the other side of the hospital. Lynette would have to be moved over there.

Although Lynette's three roommates were friendly, it was a blessing for her to move. The semi-private room proved to be a real boon when she became ill once more, a few days later. Swallowing was still extremely difficult, and she seemed to cough up every thing she tried to eat. When her temperature climbed, the doctor diagnosed pneumonia again and ordered all meals stopped and a feeding tube inserted through her nose. Liquids and antibiotics were started intravenously, and all therapy was postponed. Our spirits sank with this new setback

Lynette's temperature remained elevated for days. The doctors were puzzled and performed endless series of tests. The X-rays showed her lungs to be clear, and blood tests revealed no infectious bacteria. Another brain scan was taken.

It revealed nothing. Finally, a spinal tap was performed.

"We don't think she has meningitis, but we need another tap before we can rule it out," they informed us.

We were frightened. Could it be possible for Lynette to survive such a torturous brain surgery only to succumb to meningitis? What could possibly be worse? The nurses were excellent, especially one named Kim, who often worked overtime trying to make Lynette more comfortable. Lynette's splitting headaches were relieved with crushed Tylenol at first, until the doctor ordered all medication suspended in order to see how high the fever would go!

Lynette's illness coincided with the termination of her Decadron medication, and I suggested she might be having withdrawal symptoms. This was ruled out because she was not shaking or convulsing. We noticed a bulging in the incision area at the back of her head, but another brain scan showed no irregularity.

Back to meningitis.

Art and my sisters, Elly and Eva, took turns sitting with Lynette through the long nights, bathing her hot forehead, arms and legs. Her temperature remained high. One Sunday morning, after sitting with Lynette all night, Art noticed a bevy of doctors coming and going in a flurry of more consultations and tests. Desperate for a solution to Lynette's headaches, with pounding pain so extreme that she cried, Art demanded to know what they were doing.

"We want to do another spinal tap. We definitely suspect meningitis," answered the doctor curtly.

"Oh no, you don't. There must be a simpler answer." Art remembered how painful the previous spinal tap had been.

The procedure is to freeze the spine locally, insert a long needle into the spine and remove enough fluid for testing. The removal of even one drop of spinal fluid can cause excruciating headaches. Moreover, it is imperative to lie flat on the back for six hours after the spinal tap. This was especially painful for Lynette since pillows under her neck eased the pressure on her incision area.

Art headed for the phone and paged Dr. Miller. He told the neurosurgeon that Lynette's source of pain was obviously from the swelling at the incision. Why must she have any more needles and painful tests, he demanded.

At least now the doctors had learned to read Lynette's chart carefully. The doctor who was to perform the spinal tap was just completing his long and careful examination of the reports when Dr. Miller whisked into Lynette's room. Swiftly but gently he touched the swelling. Lynette cried out and grabbed his hand.

"Bring me a razor and syringe," he ordered.

Nurses ran at his command. In no time he had shaved a tiny area of hair, inserted the needle into the swelling and instantly filled the syringe with the gathered fluids. He did this again and again till the skin was quite flat again. So quickly did he remedy the problem that Lynette hardly noticed the pain. She was aware only of relief.

Dr. Miller explained to Art this problem was quite common a few days after brain surgery. It happens when the bone in the skull is not totally healed, causing spinal fluid to leak.

The busy surgeon left as quickly as he had come. A half hour later, Lynette's temperature had dropped a whole degree and her headache was gone. It was a few days before her temperature was normal again and Lynette got her strength back.

One morning, when she finally felt up to walking again, I took her down the hall while the staff stood and cheered her on. I fought back the tears that were always so ready to flow at the slightest provocation.

Lynette's therapy resumed and her progress was amazingly speedy. I would usually be there to take her down to the gym. There the therapist would take over while I sat and watched. Most of the patients in the walking class were elderly people recuperating from a stroke. To see my young daughter in a similar condition and straining so entirely to be successful was heartbreaking to me. Only God knows how often my one cry would be, "Lord, help her!"

Chapter Twelve

RECEIVING STRENGTH

"I am so tired of coming home to an empty house. I hate to be here by myself. You're never here, Mom. People bring us so many goodies — cakes and rolls — they're delicious, but I never have a square meal. I just snack all evening after school. I'm getting fat. Why does God do this to us?" Arlene's frustrations vented themselves and tears filled her big blue eyes.

"Why don't you come with me Saturday and spend the day at the hospital?" I suggested.

"I hate the hospital, Mom. It's so boring and all those sick people around . . . how can Lynette stand it? I just can't stay there all day."

Throughout Lynette's ordeal Arlene was undergoing struggles of her own. Left to shift for herself so much of the time, there were few opportunities to share with her parents the fears and questions that were on her mind. Frequently, she would pick up a friend and come to the hospital for a while. She had just received her driver's license and was fast learning to find her way around the city. When I returned home from the hospital, she would often be in bed or away at a school or church function.

Although I missed her and my heart ached for her, knowing there were many hurts inside her which she usually covered with a cheerful exterior, there seemed so little I could do for her. When I did attempt to talk things over with her, Arlene would retort, "You have enough problems without mine. Lynette is more important." I would try to explain to her that Lynette was not more important, her needs were simply more urgent right now. I suppose I will never know whether I chose my priorities correctly at that time, but my mind was almost totally taken up with the immediate need of the ill child.

I was always so exhausted by nighttime that I'd just drop into bed and cry myself to sleep. Occasionally, as the sun began setting later, I'd go into the garden and work off some tension. I remember planting potatoes one evening after ten o'clock. It was dark by the time I finished, but I felt good after the intense physical exercise.

Falling asleep at night was not usually a problem, but I would awake wondering why I felt so depressed. Slowly the truth would invade my mind once more. I'd have to face another day. When self-pity crept in, I'd quickly remind myself that I was not the one actually suffering. Lynette needed me to be strong. I'd pray for strength for each member of our family, whatever the needs would be that day.

For Art, who had gone back to construction after seeding. He needed motivation to work and patient wisdom to supervise his men. His normal cheerfulness, optimism, and enthusiasm were lagging.

For Cam, who had to do much of the seeding without Art this year. He needed wisdom and courage to keep going.

For Janet, mother of a hyperactive, slightly colicky baby boy. She had to be initiated into her new role without her mother or even mother-in-law nearby to help her.

For Arlene, who was struggling with her grade ten studies as well as piano theory. She was trying to cope on her own and certainly needed God's strength.

Friends would ask me, "How do you cope? How can you stand the hospital atmosphere? Don't you ever wear out?"

I was very much aware of God's strength. I was usually too exhausted or distraught for meaningful devotional times. I knew that because I was not a strong physically, emotionally, or spiritually, I depended greatly on the prayers of friends, but mostly I depended on the Lord. I was amazed at how I could relax, totally confident that the Lord made no mistakes and that

He would not allow anything to happen in my life that He and I could not handle together.

Lynette and I, together with Art, whenever he could come, would usually have a devotional time together before we said good-night. This seemed to be the highlight of the day for Lynette, and it helped me to leave her in the Lord's hands for the night.

I believed that somehow the Lord would be glorified through Lynette's suffering. If that were true, I would not interfere with His plans by complaining and crying; I wanted to allow Him to show His power through me. For that reason I was so very grateful for the thousands of prayers of people all over the world. Although the Bible college in Kelowna had closed for the summer, many students asked their home churches to pray, thus multiplying the number of prayers.

One day, I received a letter from a former roommate of Lynette's. It was Cindy Van Damme from BC, asking whether she could be of any assistance to us if she came to spend some time with us. The degree of maturity of her understanding for our situation impressed me greatly. I wrote Cindy that she was welcome if she felt she could handle Lynette's illness. Cindy called and said she would come.

We kept Cindy's arrival a secret from Lynette. One day, toward the end of June, I picked up Cindy at the airport and drove her to the Rehab. The expression on Lynette's face when Cindy walked into her room was worth the secrecy!

The two girls became inseparable. Lynette was finally discharged on June 29, 1984, exactly two months after being admitted into hospital. Her swallowing had improved rapidly and she could walk without the walker. She still wore an eye patch, but her double vision was slowly improving. Cindy helped by driving to the Rehab with Lynette, three times a week throughout July and once a week in August.

Although Lynette had been asked to be maid-of-honor at her cousin Laurie's wedding, she had to turn down the opportunity. Her walking was simply not steady enough. Instead, smartly sporting her eye patch, she wore her royal blue bridesmaid's gown, and sat at the guest book! Laurie's marriage meant an end to their carefree, girlish friendship which would have to resume on a different level. Cindy helped to fill the void that Lynette felt deeply.

The first weekend at home, Lynette developed a tingling sensation in her right side, arm, and leg. Naturally we were alarmed. Nevertheless, Dr. Miller was very sure of himself when he told Lynette there was nothing wrong with her.

"There can't be. We got all of the tumor out. It was not malignant it just can't be."

He did, however, order another CAT Scan for the following week, although we were not to receive the results for another month.

Chapter Thirteen

MORE STORM CLOUDS

"Isn't it great to be able to be going away together knowing Lynette is all right? I almost feel guilty to be so free!" I commented to Art as we left our yard. We were on our way to our annual church conference at Blumenort, about an hour's drive from home.

"Since Lynette has been home, and Cindy has been here, I've had more time to work in the garden. Have you noticed the tiger lilies blooming? Maybe it's just me, but it seems like our trees and garden have never looked greener or more lush than this summer." I was feeling more talkative than usual, but then Art and I had not had much time for talking lately.

"Look at the wheat field, Rose," Art pointed to one of our fields we were passing. "It's been years since we've had such a heavy crop. That field could run an easy 45 to 50 bushels an acre. This should be a year to get ahead on farm payments."

We stopped to pick up some friends and continued on our way.

We noticed dark clouds in the west.

"Let's hope we get some rain to cool off this hot, humid weather," someone remarked.

"Yes, we could afford some more moisture. I just hope our girls don't run into bad weather — Lynette and Cindy went swimming in Carman," I added.

"We're not worrying today, remember?" Art looked at me with a smile.

As provincial chairman of Mennonite Disaster Service, Art had been asked to give a report at the convention that afternoon. He was to issue a strong challenge for volunteers: ". . . . the U.S. has had a record number of over 700 tornadoes thus far in 1984, and MDS is making an appeal for voluntary help in many areas of the States . . . ."

Our church ladies' group was in charge of serving the "faspa," a traditional Mennonite meal of buns, meat, cheese and sweet cakes. When we had finished serving, we sat down to eat. Somebody called Art to the phone. Instinctively, I knew something terrible had happened, but which one of the children would it be?

Arlene, who was at camp?

Lynette and Cindy, who had gone swimming?

Cam, Janet, or Curtis at home?

When Art returned he was very abrupt.

"We've got to go home right away. There's a tornado in Rosenort. Brother Jake's machine shed blew away."

"That's just a quarter-mile from our farm! It couldn't hit us, could it?"

"I'm not sure. I tried to call Cam, but there's no answer. The telephone operator told me not to bother phoning. She said, 'Just go home!' Come on, let's go."

As we hurried home in the driving rain, I kept thinking, "It couldn't happen to us. We've had our share of problems. . . . it happened to Job — it could happen to us."

"I just pray the girls are safe," I said. "If they went to Carman, they'll have run smack into that tornado!"

The closer we got to Rosenort, the heavier our hearts became.

Fifteen miles from home, we noticed the heavy crops were flattened. Five miles from home, most houses and sheds had the shingles shaved off. One mobile home was missing. Large steel grain bins were toppled over, some crumpled up like paper. The closer we got to our farm, the worse the damage looked.

As in the story of Job, God sent us a messenger to break the news. A mile and a half from home, our brother-in-law Henry stopped us. He handed us snapshots he had already taken.

"Here's one of Cam's house." A garage wall was caved in.

"This is Jake Cornelsens' house." The machine shed and car garage were both sitting in his living room.

"This is your farm!"

I couldn't look. I had to know about the girls first. Were they all right? Had they been at home?

"Oh yes, the girls were at home when it hit. They're all right!"

"Oh, thank-you, Lord. Then I can handle the rest!"

A mile from home we could see that the entire row of tall poplar trees was bent eastward. Upon reaching the yard, I began to cry. Our beautiful spreading poplar in the middle of our front lawn was pitifully broken up. Over half of it had been brutally torn from the trunk, and what was left standing had most of the limbs broken. Branches were strewn everywhere.

The barn's hip roof had been cleanly lifted off and dumped into the middle of the yard. Art gave a hard laugh when Cam came to greet us.

"Well, the job's been done for us. We wanted to change that roof anyway!" Art remarked dryly.

Two of our large steel bins had toppled over; one was draped across the disc, crushing its fertilizer box. The bulk fuel tanks were scattered across the yard like match boxes.

Miraculously, the house had been spared. Although two large elm trees just ten feet away had snapped, the house suffered only one cracked windowpane.

Carefully, I stepped over scattered debris; broken boards, branches, straw and shingles on my way into the house.

The girls greeted me tearfully. Cindy was busy mopping up the floor.

"Are you all right? Where were you when the tornado hit — why were you home?" My questions tumbled out one after the other.

"We're OK, I guess — but we were just petrified!" Lynette said tremulously.

Lynette and Cindy had seen the black clouds on their way to Carman and decided to turn back. At home, Cindy had driven the car into the shed as a precaution. While she was walking back to the house, the wind had suddenly picked up, and she had to struggle to get indoors. Once inside, she was shocked to look out the window and see the big trees snap like twigs. When the front door blew open, and Cindy was unable to close it, the girls decided to run for the basement. This was no easy task with Lynette needing assistance.

After things quieted down, Cindy ran for the phone to call Cam. At once Cam and Janet, whose barbecue supper with their friends had been rudely interrupted by the storm, came over to console the girls. Their friends, Brad and Laverna followed. Although the end wall of Cam's garage was caved in, there was no immediate emergency at his house.

While Janet and Laverna busily cleaned out our truck cab, which was filled with straw and mud, Cam and Brad drove around the neighborhood to check who needed immediate help. Jake Cornelsen's children had been home alone and were badly frightened and in need of comfort.

Art alerted the surrounding communities for MDS help. With local help, he set up an office in the Rosenort Fire Hall and organized the volunteers who began to arrive immediately. An SOS on the radio brought power generators to livestock farmers. I called some ladies and organized them to feed the work crews that would be coming the next day.

Only hours after exclaiming over the promising harvest, our beautiful bumper crops were completely flattened out.

Late that night the phone rang.

"Hi, Mom? What's happening out there?"

It was Arlene. She was away as a junior counsellor at Red Rock Bible Camp, about 125 miles from home.

"Lots of excitement out here today," I answered.

"I saw Uncle Jake's house on TV," she began to cry.

"Everybody's fine, Arlene. How are you?"

"I'm worried. Mom, I was so scared when I saw the news. How badly is our farm damaged? Do you need me? May I came home? There's a bus going to Winnipeg tomorrow morning."

I told her the extent of damage on our farm and assured her we'd manage all right without her.

"I'm useless here now, Mom. I really want to come home for a day or so," she begged.

"All right, if it makes you feel better, come on home. What time will you be in Winnipeg?"

The borrowed generator had enough power to keep the barn fans going and also gave us a light in the house. The girls took a flashlight upstairs when they went to bed.

Janet had put Curtis to sleep in Cindy's bed, so Cindy crawled in with Lynette. Cam and Janet had gone home to wipe up water in their bedroom, where rain had streamed in through a window that had popped. Being a light sleeper, Curtis awoke crying when the girls talked together in bed. It took me a while to croon him to back to sleep. I checked on the girls before going back downstairs.

"Are you going to get any sleep tonight?" I asked.

"I'm afraid to close my eyes, Mom. I keep seeing those trees bending. I was so sure the house would fly away," Lynette confided, shaking again. "And I keep thinking of Wade (Jake Cornelsen's 14-year old son). He could have been killed when that granary came rolling after him!

"It's a miracle that he got into the house on time," said Cindy, also shivering in the darkness.

"Yes, it is a miracle. The important thing is that nobody was hurt. God protected you and I'm so glad about that," I said.

"But, Mom, why did God let this happen to us? We've had enough trouble without a tornado. How does God expect us to handle this?" Lynette asked.

"If I could answer that, I'd be the wisest person in the world! I don't know why or how. I figure it out like this: if the problem is so great that I can't handle it, I tell God it's His problem. He'll have to handle it for me. Somehow there will be help, and we'll make it. To tell you the truth, I don't have the ambition to clean up this yard. I'm tired of our troubles, too, but I'm not going to let the devil get me down. We can't quit now!"

I was fighting depression and hopelessness, and a nagging dread as to what the future held for us, but I could not afford to let the girls know how close to despair I was.

I prayed with the girls and left them more relaxed. The events of the day had exhausted them. They would sleep.

We were almost surprised to see the sun shining the next morning. Crews of workers arrived early to help with the clean-up, but frustrations set in when progress was hampered by a constant stream of sightseers. Trucks and front-end loaders were kept busy moving the remains of the shattered roof on the yard. Chain saws cut away broken trees, and before evening our huge poplar was reduced to something resembling a totem pole.

MDS volunteers faithfully showed up in Rosenort for the next several weeks. The amount of debris hauled from our yard totalled 47 large grain-truck loads. Our barn was soon dressed with a new shingled roof, and the steel granaries were repaired and back in place. Even the crops were making a startling come-back. Cautiously, we grew more optimistic. Cindy began to enjoy Manitoba once again, and Lynette was making clear progress.

The first Sunday in August dawned warm and clear. We had not had too many opportunities for fun that summer, so we packed a lunch and our swimsuits and headed for Grand Beach! It proved to be a good decision, but a 100,000 other people thought so too. There was a record-breaking crowd on the beach that day, but we enjoyed ourselves thoroughly. The sun was hot, and the water was calm and warm. The girls were in their element, trying to outdo one another in getting the darkest suntan.

By 4:00 p.m. Lynette was tired, however, and we packed our things and left.

Janet's sister and brother-in-law, Donna and Gord, were visiting from BC, so we invited them all over to our house for a late supper. We had hardly finished eating, when the sky suddenly clouded over and lightning flashed. Curious to see what was developing, we ran outside to find the sky a heavy mass of roaring, blackish green clouds, churning and boiling angrily.

It was more than the cold breeze that made me shiver. What were we in for now? I didn't have to wait long for my answer. Giant drops of rain came pounding down as we all scooted into the house for cover.

"I've never seen anything like that before," remarked Donna. "Those clouds look awesome."

We heard the raindrops change to clattering balls of ice.

Cindy began to wail, "Head for the basement, everybody." She grabbed Lynette and together they hurried downstairs.

The rest of us stood by the open door, fascinated by nature's bizarre display of power.

It suddenly dawned on Gord that his new car was sitting outside, getting dented by the hail. He was out the door before we realized where he was headed.

"Come back here, Gord, you'll get killed," I yelled after him. After just minutes, the lawn was completely covered with a thick layer of ice, and the hail was still pelting down heavily. Gord never ventured more than two steps outside however, before he ducked back indoors.

"What about the windows upstairs? Are they closed?" Art asked. We both dashed up to check.

"I guess the crops will be totalled now." The despairing tone of Art's voice tore at my heart. I went up to him and he put his arms around me tightly. "What can we do? We don't even have any insurance on the crops."

"We can pray. God knows we need the crops!"

"O, Lord, stop the hail. Protect the crops, please!" Art prayed aloud.

But the hail continued. Never had we seen it hail this long before — a full thirty minutes! We knew that the canola and wheat on the fields around the farm would be completely destroyed, but we hoped that our fields several miles west would have been spared. We would have to wait until morning to inspect the damage.

We slept very little that night. When dawn lit up the world, we went out to view the ravages of the storm. It seemed devastation was everywhere.

For the second time that summer our sad looking trees had lost their leaves. The canola field was reduced to pulp. A few broken stems stuck out of the soggy wheat field. Driving to our property west of the farm, we discovered the hail had followed a path identical to that of the tornado four weeks earlier. A thousand acres of our crops were destroyed.

This loss was harder to bear than the tornado damage. Buildings could be repaired, but with very little crop insurance, we were financially ruined.

On top of illness, we would now have severe financial problems as well. How could we manage to make ends meet?

What was God trying to do? Were we such slow learners that He had to keep hammering at us? What did He want of us? Why did God allow so much pain in our lives?

As I pondered these questions, I became almost excited to anticipate how God would act: would He work a miracle? At any rate, we would learn to depend entirely on Him to see us through.

> Beloved, be not surprised at the fiery ordeal among you, which comes upon you for your testing, as though some strange thing were happening to you; but to the degree that you share the sufferings of Christ, keep on rejoicing; so that also at the revelation of His glory you may rejoice with exultation. 1 Peter 4: 12,13

> . . . God will now not allow you to be tempted beyond that you are able . . . . 1 Corinthians 10:13

But we have this treasure in earthen vessels, that the excellency of the power may be of God, and not of us. We are troubled on every side, yet not distressed; we are perplexed, but not in despair; persecuted but no forsaken; cast down, but not destroyed; always bearing about in the body the dying of the Lord Jesus, that the life also of Jesus might be made manifest in our body. 2 Corinthians 4:7-10

Chapter Fourteen

COLLEGE AGAIN

Therapy at the Rehab Centre had been very successful for Lynette. The last week in August, she was given various tests, such as running the length of the gym, walking backwards, doing sit-ups, performing hand and arm strengthening and finer control exercises, and speech therapy. It was decided she did not need to come back, other than for monthly checkups.

Lynette and Cindy had been making plans to attend Steinbach Bible College, 40 miles from home, in the fall. This would be an excellent pastime for Lynette while she was still regaining her strength. Cindy would be able to continue her studies and still assist Lynette whenever needed.

Lynette's gait was somewhat unsteady, especially where the ground was soft or uneven. Her voice was very weak and hoarse — described by some as a sensual whisper — so that Cindy frequently did Lynette's speaking for her. At school, Cindy would also be able to take notes in class for Lynette, since her right hand was too weak to write.

Earlier in summer we had promised to pay the girls' tuition, but after the hailstorm, we could not see how we could possibly afford it. The girls kept on praying. One day, a week before school opened, I noticed Lynette had lain down in our bedroom after supper.

"Are you sick?" I asked.

"No," her voice was muffled by the pillow.

"What's the matter?"

"I guess I'm getting discouraged again. This morning I prayed for a specific answer from God about attending school. I prayed that if Ben Eidse (president of SBC) would visit us today, it would mean God wants me to go to school. That's not asking too much, is it? After all, Mr. Eidse knows we're interested and he's visited other young people around here. He hasn't shown up today, so I guess I'll have to make new plans."

What comfort could I offer? Before I managed to frame a reply, I had to answer a knock on the door.

"Mr. Eidse!" was all I could say.

"May I come in?" he asked.

"Of course, come on in."

Lynette was so astonished when she came into the kitchen that she just stared. I finally got my wits together and pulled out chairs around the dining room table.

"Do you realize that you were specifically guided over here by God today?" I asked Mr. Eidse. After I explained about Lynette's prayer, it was his turn to marvel.

"My car broke down a few miles from here yesterday. I came to pick it up and decided to drop in on my way. Yes, this is definitely more than a coincidence," he remarked.

Mr. Eidse encouraged both girls to put in their applications and trust the Lord for the finances. Of course, the girls applied and were accepted. It was marvelous to see their needs being met, especially Cindy's. Friends supplied her with linens and bedding, toiletries and money. Our church helped with her board and tuition.

Those fall months were Lynette's happiest during her illness. She was able to keep busy and fill her time usefully. She developed friendships on a deep level with many girls whom she would never have met otherwise.

Given the opportunity to present her testimony during chapel time, Lynette helped the student body to understand her handicaps. Through Cindy's voice she delivered the following:

> I just want to take this time to explain a few things to you about myself. I can't give this speech myself because my voice is quite soft and chances are nobody would hear me.

As a lot of you know, I began my second year at Okanagan Bible College last year. I really learned a lot there and loved it. Two months into the year, I had to leave to see a doctor here in Manitoba. I had a brain scan done, but I didn't fully realize how serious it was. I was told I had a brain tumor and it would be hard to get at because it was located right in the middle of all my nerves. They couldn't promise to get all of it but they'd do their best.

I had my first operation a year ago on November 1st. As they said, they couldn't get all of it, but they got enough to do a biopsy and we were all *very* relieved when they said it was not malignant. They couldn't cut it all out without making me handicapped in some way. They thought they could get the rest with cobalt treatments. I began a series of 30 treatments at the Manitoba Cancer Society in Winnipeg. When I was finally done, they told us that it was all gone. We were ecstatic! It had been hard on the whole family, and now it was finally over!

For some reason I couldn't believe the tumor was really totally gone, so Mom called my doctor to make sure. Sure enough, we had misunderstood! All the swelling and pressure had disappeared, but the tumor was still there.

A few months later, in April, my right cheek and my whole right side started to go numb.

My cheek was really paralyzed. My smile even drooped! Needless to say, I was really scared! My doctor just took one look at me and knew I'd need another operation. He said it was very serious and they'd probably handicap me in some way. Without the operation I would die in only a matter of months.

I had my second operation in May. This time I almost died because they moved me out of Intensive Care too soon. I couldn't breathe, and I'm sure that if my sister-in-law hadn't made me keep breathing, I would have been gone. Finally, I just passed out. When I woke up, I had a bunch of tubes in me and an oxygen mask over my face.

I had to learn to walk, write, swallow and eat all over again. For over a month, I didn't have one bite of food! I was in the hospital and Rehab for nine weeks. That beat what the doctor predicted! It was a very hard time for me, and I thought that if one more person would tell me to have patience, I'd just explode! I learned a lot during that time. I often just gave up. I couldn't figure out why God would allow me to be in so much pain. I had so much time to think about it, but I learned that He isn't punishing me for something I did, but rather, that this might be helping somebody else in his Christian walk.

I often said that if just one person is helped by this, then it'll be worth it. I shouldn't even be here, but I believe and am convinced that it's because of people's prayers for me that I can go to school.

I still get frustrated a lot of the time because I find it hard to communicate with people, and I would ask you to pray for me, especially for my eye. During my last operation they stretched my eye nerve, causing double vision. That's why I wear a patch on it.

If it doesn't get better on its own, I'll have to
have surgery on it.
I thank God that I have come this far, and
I thank those who have prayed for me.
Thanks.

While Lynette and Cindy were settling into their routine
for the winter, other changes were happening in the family.

Arlene's time at camp helped her to mature spiritually, as
well as allowing her to escape some of the emotional stresses at
home.

During a local rodeo, Arlene also worked as a
photographer's helper and learned some valuable lessons in
employment. Most importantly, it meant she was able to earn
some money for herself and gave her a good feeling of self-
worth.

Little Curtis had won himself a very special spot in all our
hearts. We were almost as excited as Cam and Janet when his
first tooth popped through and when he learned to shake his
finger at himself and say "bad" when he touched a forbidden
houseplant. When the tornado blew the roof off the barn, a lit-
ter of kittens was uncovered: how Curtis loved the scrawny
little orphans! He'd cuddle them in his arms, until we'd have to
rescue them from his intense squeezes. Despite his slight build,
Curtis was a wiry, strong baby, eager to explore and learn new
things. He'd squeal with joy when Grandpa would take him for
a ride on the garden tractor or big grain truck. Reading stories,
singing action songs, or relaxing on the garden swing with
Grandma were also fun times. What a blessing he was to us! He
was an active little tyke and we were not surprised when he got
tired of crawling and began to run on his own at nine months
old! Grandpa's special name for him became "Tiger."

Another change that fall was our decision to move off the
farm and into town. The ball had been set in motion when Cam
sold 80 acres of his land in order to buy our home 80. We
decided to trade houses. Janet was eagerly looking forward to

the move and she had plans to redecorate the farm house. Curtis would have the whole farmyard to explore and Cam would be around the yard, choring his hogs in the barn. That November the exchange was made.

One morning in early December the phone rang. It was the dean of women at the SBC. I tensed.

"Hello, Mrs. Cornelsen? I'm calling for Lynette. She just wanted you to know that she's not feeling too well. She was doing her daily gratis work this morning of wrapping cutlery in napkins, when she noticed she was continually dropping things. Her hands seem to be getting weaker and she's scared." I could tell the dean was upset, too.

"Does she want to come home?" I asked.

"No, I think she just wanted you to be aware of how things are going. We'll call you if she gets worse."

"Thanks for calling. Keep in touch and just tell her we love her and that we'll be there as soon as you need us. I suppose she'll be home this weekend?"

"Yes, she has the car here, so she said she'd be home early on Friday."

"Great!"

My heart sank as I hung up the phone. This was the first sign of a relapse since her surgery. She'd had some bad headaches when she started studying but they had stopped and we hoped they had been caused by eye strain. Her eye had improved remarkably to the extent that she could wear her contact lenses once more. Her hair had grown back, and she was able to wear it curled and shoulder length. Her last CAT scan had shown a slight shadow which the surgeon believed was scar tissue. A follow-up at the Rehab had revealed all her movements slightly weaker than in August, but Dr. Miller remained optimistic. Upon his advice, Lynette decided to go for job training after Christmas, a program offered by the Crippled Children and Adults Society.

I picked up the phone and called Art at his job. He had just started on the construction of a new church in the neighborhood.

I could sense his shock in his tone of voice. He had been so full of hope for Lynette's complete recovery.

On Friday, Lynette arrived home in time for lunch. I was shocked when I saw her come in the door. It was only a week since I'd last seen her. Had my eyes been blind to the obvious change, or had it happened so quickly?

Dark circles around her eyes accentuated the high cheekbones. Had her cheeks been hollow like that before? Was I imagining her dragging her right foot? I hoped so! She had obviously lost weight about 20 pounds since summer but she had looked good that way.

"Hi! Welcome home! How was the drive home?" I asked. She was still nervous about driving but loved the feeling of independence in getting around by herself.

"Noth thoo bad. I'm lucky there's tho little sthnow. Cindy didn't come along this weekend. She's planning tho go back home to BC at Christmaths." Lynette looked weary.

"How are you feeling?" I asked the question that Lynette had come to hate but which needed to be asked.

"Thired, justh therribly thired, I'd like tho resth before lunch."

I helped her carry her suitcase to her room. The slur in her speech alarmed me, but Lynette insisted she was all right. She spent the weekend studying for exams. She didn't have to be back at school until noon Monday so she stayed home till that morning. It was a cold, blustery morning and I offered to drive her back.

"I can manage to drive, Mom. Don't treat me like an invalid. I'm not totally handicapped, you know!"

"But it's starting to snow. What if you run into a blizzard?"

"Mom, did we ever tell you that you worry too much?" Lynette was losing patience with me.

"All right, but leave as soon as you can, and wear your toque and scarf and snow boots . . . ."

"Yes, mother!"

She was ready to leave, and I noticed she was wearing her running shoes.

"Lynette, you have to wear your boots. You already have trouble with your legs. You can't risk chilling them," I advised chidingly.

"They're so heavy," she complained, but obligingly pulled them on. She would have left without saying good-bye, but I reached out and gave her a hug.

"Please drive carefully. The storm is picking up."

"An accident might be the best answer," was her angry response as she wiped away tears of frustration.

"Bye, Lynette, I love you," I called after her as she dragged her feet to the car. "Call me when you get there."

I closed the door and went to my bedroom to talk to my heavenly Father. My burdened heart was too heavy to bear alone.

"O Lord, keep her safe. Comfort her, she is hurting and is so miserable. I can't help her, but she is my child and I hurt for her. I know you understand because your Son hurt, too. How it must have pained you when you had to forsake Him, and He had to face the suffering and death by Himself. Thank-you for your love and understanding. But do help Lynette right now! Amen."

Half an hour later a full-scale Manitoba blizzard was whipping up a zero visibility storm. The phone rang. It was Art.

"Rose, don't let Lynette go anywhere in this storm," he warned.

"I hate to tell you this, but she's left already," I answered.

"Then we'll just have to pray for her safety. Let me know if you hear from her."

I promised to call Art the minute I heard from Lynette. I'd barely hung up when the phone rang again.

"Hi, Mom, I just wanted to tell you I got here OK," Lynette's whispering voice had never sounded sweeter. "And, Mom, thanks for loving and caring and praying, and for being you. I love you! Pray for my exam this afternoon."

I breathed a thank-you to my Father! When I phoned her later that week, she told me that she was allowed to write her exams in her dormitory room because the walk to the school was simply too strenuous for her. That weekend Cindy came home with her. She was not planning to come back to school so this was her last visit with us before she flew home. On Sunday evening we had a special Christmas candle-light supper. We exchanged gifts and had a happy time together before driving her to the airport.

Chapter Fifteen

SURGERY #3

On Christmas Eve, our family all attended the Sunday school program, where the highlight was watching Janet and Curtis join the mothers' class in singing a lullaby.

Janet loved to show off her little boy, and everyone readily forgave her when she'd proudly ask, "Isn't he cute?"

When we came home Lynette burst into tears. "I won't ever be normal again," she cried.

How I wanted to tell her she was wrong! In my eyes, both my daughters were equally and beautifully charming. Lynette's eyes had a haunting brightness, however, which told me far more than the doctor's brain scans could.

Our Warkentin Christmas family-gathering turned out to be a painful one. Lynette's walking was deteriorating quickly and her smile was so crooked that everybody was shocked. On December 27, we took Lynette to see our family doctor in St. Boniface. He ordered another CAT scan and sent us home. That evening Lynette hyperventilated and thought she was dying. We calmed her down, but I threw a blanket on the floor beside her bed and watched her all night. Even in her sleep her breathing was very uneven. Something had to be done!

My sister, Elly, was very faithful in keeping the absent family members informed of the events in our household. The following which she wrote covered the nightmarish happenings of the subsequent weeks:

January 11, 1985
Rosenort, Manitoba

Dear family,

Hi! We trust your holidays have been more than you could have wished for.

I'm sure all of you are waiting for some details of the latest news on Lynette's condition, before and after surgery. December 25 we had our family gathering at the school. Art, Rose and Arlene came at the appointed time, bringing their foodstuffs, etc. Rose went back home, saying Lynette wasn't feeling well enough to come with the rest of them, but that they'd both arrive for supper and the evening.

When they came, Lynette needed an arm for support in walking. We thought her voice had become fainter also. I think most of us were shocked to see her in such a weakened state. All fall Rose had said (whenever asked, never making a big fuss about it) that despite the doctors' numerous reports of Lynette getting better, she was getting weaker especially, one side. Lynette insisted on finishing her semester at SBC, at times crying for sheer frustration at her limitations and increasing weakness, at other times grinning at our amazement when she appeared without her eye patch. She was due to get glasses, although contact lenses were her goal. Her scan in November showed that the "shadow" area hadn't changed at all; in fact, she showed remarkable improvement in many previous problems.

"Be assured, Mr. and Mrs. Cornelsen, her tingling sensations which are becoming more apparent, are most likely severed nerve endings in the state of healing. Her weakness could be scar tissue becoming thicker and pressing in on some tender spots. Her improvements and the scan are both very encouraging." To live with such contradictions. Rose once told me she'd just given Lynette a vigorous massage to try and get some circulation warmth into her hands and feet, so that she could try and get some sleep. Surely, if this were nerves repairing themselves, it wouldn't be cutting off circulation! But, "be positive" was the doctors' message. Who were we to argue?

On December 23rd, we invited the Cornelsens and Mom over for a Christmas dinner, but they declined, saying Lynette wasn't up to it. I'll always wonder why it never occurred to us to pack up our food and share it over there! Mom came and Pam brought a friend from church. They went to see Lynette later on, and both were very quiet when they came home. They just hadn't realized Lynette was having such a hard time. How had she ever finished a whole semester at school — in fact, driven a car to and from Steinbach?

On December 27th, the Cornelsens went to see Dr. Kirk, asking him to keep Lynette in hospital for testing. He advised she'd be more comfortable at home, since during holiday time very little was done in the labs or elsewhere.

On December 28th, they phoned Mom to say they were taking Lynette to the hospital in Winnipeg. They'd all been napping Friday noon, with Lynette on the living room couch.

She was feeling particularly bad and wanted to get to her own room down the hall but found herself helpless to do so — not even to crawl. That was it! She was hospitalized at St. Boniface, where on Monday, December 31, they did a scan. When we asked Lynette later on whether the results were what she had anticipated, she said, "I sort of expected the doctor would say there was another tumor — but just one, not two."

Everyone keeps saying how well Art, Rose and Lynette are taking everything. Rose exclaimed yesterday, "Us peaceful about it? It's nice to know we give an image like that, but . . .!" The doctors gave them an ultimatum: a slight chance for recovery with another operation, or two weeks to two months left for Lynette without one. Lynette herself (after some deep discussion and prayer with her parents) said, "Go for it."

Art and Rose decided to stay on hand at the hospital,even through the night. That last week, from Monday to Thursday, anyone could see how fast she was weakening. When she was first brought to Health Sciences Centre, she was put into the same intensive care room where she'd fought so hard last time — she found that very hard at first. As she got weaker Lynette became more appreciative of the constant presence of nurses. She was moved to a semi-private room for one and half days or so, but the night before surgery she was back in ICU. I was asked to stay for that night, but Lynette wanted one of her parents on hand regardless, so we took all shifts. By morning, we were convinced that, in her condition, if she came through surgery at all, it would be only through the prayers of all Christians interceding. Lynette said on Tuesday, "At other times, I've had reserves of strength. This time I have nothing. If I make it, it'll be by the prayers of others."

At 7:15 a.m. they came to get Lynette from the room; Art and Rose saw her off as far as they could go with her. They found this very hard, knowing there were still hours of preparations when she'd be awake and in need of loving support. Sitting at the breakfast cafeteria table, we had special prayer for this hour of need.

Art had reserved a room at the new Ronald McDonald House for parents and they were already changing off shifts sleeping and sitting with Lynette, so he took me there to keep Arlene company and catch some sleep. Sleep???

People came and went all day. By 4:00-5:00 Rose said they could start asking for some news. They'd started late, however (after 10:00 a.m.) and were right in the midst of microscopic surgery and it would be a few hours yet. Just knowing she'd made it so far and that they were proceeding according to plan was reassuring. Later on, we all admitted we hadn't really thought she could stand this operation and we were waiting to be told that. Pam and I left at 5:30 p.m. so all the rest is hearsay. It was torture for us here at home, so we could just imagine the drawn-out agony of the family.

At 11:15 p.m. Janet and Laurie were on the yard, bringing Mom home. At 12:00 midnight I couldn't stand not knowing any longer yet I could imagine everyone jumping in the waiting room if I were to call. Call I did, however. "Right on cue!" Art answered. They'd just talked with the doctor, who said Lynette was bypassing "Recovery" and going into ICU, where they could see her. Moments later they did and she recognized them right away. What was stunning to everyone was that they had removed four satellite tumors in the one "spinal" spot or as they said later "one big one interwoven," and left the second one untouched, seeing Lynette had had all she could take. We could praise God she'd come through as well as she had. She was hooked up to a respirator and heart machine the first few days, the tracheotomy taking care of her swallowing and breathing difficulties.

Today it's a week later. I went in to see Lynette after 6:00 p.m. She'd been there a whole day without the machine, which makes her very tired from the effort of breathing. I felt it had been a day of progress, and I walked in confidently, thanking God for an optimistic outlook. I had barely taken her hand and touched her shoulder (she lies quietly with her eyes closed most of the time), when she began crying. I wiped her mouth and she kept saying "suction," so the nurse cleared all that up. She tried telling me something: "hurts very much . . . ," but I couldn't make it out. She finally twisted her mouth in frustration, and slowly stopped sobbing. I could have screamed for sheer compassion (much good that would do!), but all that came out was a quiet "Oh, Lynette, I'm sorry I'm so dumb! I don't get it, so don't waste your strength on it." She said yes to my suggestion of prayer. After that and some singing, she was totally quiet, looking absolutely exhausted. I left (I feel now I chickened out) saying her mom was waiting to come in and that at least she could read her needs better than I could. I felt thoroughly discouraged after what had really been a "good," productive day. If I felt like that, what about Art and Rose? And Lynette herself? Her recovery period is stretching out endlessly, with more surgery possible after that.

Art and Rose have been under tremendous strain this last while. There is no end in sight yet. Their doctor finally made an appointment to see them this morning after Rose did some phoning around yesterday. I know how anxious they have been to hear all about the predictions, facts, possibilities, lab reports, pathology, etc. so this morning is a time of much needed prayer. A lot of future planning will rest on today's report. Our hearts are heavy, and yet Christ is not being glorified by negative attitudes. It seems there's an atmosphere of genuine spiritual strength being evidenced, with a willingness to accept God's way, whatever it is, including hurts, tears, questions, even a switching off of emotions at times. The Lord is in the midst of it. Cornelsens must be special to Him right now (and who would ever *volunteer* for that position?). He's fulfilling part of His plan, like it or not. All of us, as family, have a more important part than ever in praying.

There's so much left unsaid, but you're getting the main picture, as it stands now. Why don't you fill out a page of questions and I'll see they get answered. Art and Rose are so involved right now; their minds are totally preoccupied. And while you're at it — Arlene needs an extra dose of love, appreciation and attention. She copes super well, but she is still a teenager with great needs emotionally and spiritually. Write and assure her of your prayers and concerns.

Cam attends U of M classes, studying agriculture. Janet is her cheerful, optimistic self, enjoying being a mother, etc. Art spends days (this week) supervising the construction of the Pleasant Valley Church; evenings he goes to visit Rose and Lynette.

Have to go. I promise to answer all letters immediately, even get Art or Rose to add to it.

Love,

Johnny & Elly

Chapter Sixteen

NEW YEAR'S EVE

It was New Year's Eve and it had been a grueling day. Art and I had been with Lynette since morning. I took her for another CAT scan at noon, and later that afternoon the doctors gave Art and me the grim news that there were two new tumors. Surgery would prolong her life, perhaps up to a year, although months was more realistic. The choice of whether or not to have surgery was ours.

"No, it is not our choice. It must be Lynette's. I cannot imagine living through the horrors of another operation. Lynette must choose whether it's worth it," I told the doctors.

In Lynette's room the doctor gently held her hand as he explained her choices.

"You mean it's either surgery or death? That's no choice! Go for it," she said bravely. When the doctor left, however, she began to shake with fear.

"Dad, would you phone Pastor Stan to come in? He's always so comforting and knows just what to say when I'm scared," Lynette begged.

"Certainly, and I'll call Arlene, too. I promised to let her know what was happening here. I'll let her know we'll be home late."

Art had been gone only a few minutes when who should walk in, but Pastor Stan and his wife! God had answered Lynette's desire immediately. Before they call I will answer and while they are yet speaking I will hear (Isaiah 65:24). He knew how much we all needed comfort at this time.

We stayed with Lynette until she finally relaxed and was able to settle down for the night. When we arrived home, it was midnight. We were exhausted physically and emotionally and were longing for sleep.

Upon entering our house, I sensed something wasn't right. I spied a note on the kitchen counter.

> Dear Mom and Dad,
> I've gone to the New Year's Party I told you about. I know you didn't want me to go, but I couldn't stay home alone after your phone call.
> Love, Arlene

Dread and fear had weighed down on me all day, but now it burst into full-scale panic. Why? Other kids went to New Year's parties, so why was I so afraid for Arlene? Was Lynette's illness making me so paranoid that Arlene would never be able to live a normal, independent life?

It was after midnight and time for a 16-year old to be home, I reasoned. I went to the phone and dialed.

"Hello, may I speak to Arlene, please? What do you mean, she's not there? When did she leave? Do you know where she was going? OK. Thanks."

Art had been silent through all this. He had always been one to maintain that our kids were trained to be responsible, and I thought I felt his disapproval of my action. Nonetheless, I dialed again.

"Hello, is Arlene there? No? Hasn't been there at all tonight? OK. Have a good night!" I hung up the phone and felt Art's eyes on me.

"Where is she?" he asked finally.

"I don't know, but I think the first guy lied to me. I believe he knows, but why would he lie?"

I called several of Arlene's friends. She had been in touch with them earlier but wasn't there now. Art could see I wouldn't rest until Arlene was home, and by now he began to have suspicions of his own.

"I'll get her," he said and was gone.

Relieved, I prepared for bed. An hour went by. Why did it take so long? I ran to the window with every passing car. There had never been so much traffic at this hour of the night.

Finally, I heard the garage door open and a second car drive onto our yard. Good friends of ours came in, ahead of Art.

"She's going to be all right. We just came to tell you she'll be all right," they kept repeating. I ran to open the door for Art. He was carrying Arlene in his arms. She was unconscious.

"What happened? Someone tell me what's happened." I couldn't believe what I was seeing.

After we had settled her in bed, Art explained how he had found her. At the party, the kids had insisted that Arlene wasn't there, but Art had noticed their furtive glances toward the basement door.

"Step aside, I'm going to search the house," Art had demanded.

"All right, All right, she's in the laundry room."

Having never seen any of our children drunk before, the sight of Arlene slouching in a corner on the floor, completely besotted, was almost more than Art could bear, especially after the day's awful experience with Lynette at the hospital.

"O my God, am I going to lose both daughters?" Art cried. "Where did she get the liquor? What did she drink? Why did you let her drink so much?"

The kids looked on helplessly as Art picked her up.

He placed Arlene on the back seat of the car. Not knowing what or how much she had been drinking, and having very little knowledge of liquor, he decided to stop in at our church, where a watchnight service was just ending. It was there that he met our friends who offered to come over and help.

Arlene lay so very still and her color was so gray that I began to fear she was suffering from more than intoxication. What if there were drugs involved? I called my doctor. He advised us to keep an eye on her until she woke up. If she didn't wake up by early morning, he advised, we were to bring her into the hospital.

It was a long, lonely vigil. It was also a time of deep soul searching, when I talked to the Lord constantly.

"O Lord, I don't know why we have to go through this on top of everything else. What are you trying to teach me? I'm willing to give up Lynette by now, but I cannot give up Arlene as well. Not yet, anyway. Please help her pull through and let her learn a lesson from this. Help me somehow to get through to her, to be able to spend more time with her — whatever it takes, Lord, to meet her needs.

"Help us again . . . ."

At 7:00 a.m. there was still no response from Arlene. I began to make phone calls to her friends, trying to discover whether anyone was aware of drugs or the amount of alcohol Arlene had taken. I should have expected the vague answers.

An hour later, Arlene slowly began to stir. As her eyes groggily focused on me, she began to cry.

"But I love her so much! I don't want her to die! I'm sorry, Mom, I'm so sorry. I didn't mean to hurt you, but I can't take it," she sobbed.

Although I had promised Lynette I'd be back to see her in the morning, I decided to stay home while Art and my sister went to the hospital.

The incident was a turning point in our relationship with Arlene. It became very obvious to us that we had neglected Arlene, for whatever legitimate reason. She was obviously frightened, not only of losing Lynette, but of life in general. Any teenager needs attention: how much more Arlene, given the circumstances? We realized the necessity to communicate with each other much more freely.

True to His word, God worked with us in this situation for good.

Chapter Seventeen

ANOTHER BIRTHDAY

I wasn't at all sure if I could survive the pain of seeing Lynette go through another torturous surgery, especially since the doctors did not give us any hope of a complete recovery, only a possible extension of life.

Somehow we came through those days. I had to forget about my fear of all the sickness and death in the Intensive Care Unit: Lynette's excruciating pain was the only thing we could deal with for the time being. She could not breathe on her own and her heart was very weak. One of her lungs had collapsed during surgery, her voice was useless because of the tracheotomy, and her throat was paralyzed once again, as well as the right side of her face. It was a miracle that she lived through the surgery, never mind the following 72 critical hours. This time the doctors were careful to keep her in the ICU until all danger was passed — a period of 10 days.

The care Lynette received was excellent. Her every wish was granted. Ever so slowly her strength returned, and the machines were gradually removed. In three weeks, she was able to have the trachtube removed, and she slowly began to eat on her own. A week later she was transferred to the Rehab, where she learned once more to walk with a walker before graduating to a "quad cane."

During her first walking lesson in the gym, I watched anxiously from the sidelines. As usual, the sight of Lynette's intense determination and painful effort to overcome her handicaps was enough to break my heart. I noticed that the Rehab doctor was also watching. He came over to where I was sitting.

"You know, Lynette shouldn't be here," he began.

"Pardon me?" I asked in surprise.

"She shouldn't be wasting time here," he said pointedly.

"What do you mean, 'wasting time'?"

"Don't you know she has only a short time left to live?" he asked, looking at me as if I were extremely naive.

Anger rushed through me. How dare a doctor ask anybody a question like that? How insensitive could a professional get? Never, throughout the entire course of Lynette's illness, had anybody been so heartless.

"Yes, of course, I know her condition is terminal, but I was told she might have a year. Surely, it pays to learn to walk for whatever length of time she has."

"Perhaps, but she should spend her last days at home. With a malignant tumor, the end could be very fast."

"Are you sure you've read her charts correctly?" I asked. After all, we had experienced that before! "We were told very definitely it was not malignant."

"Oh, I thought it was! I'll have to check once more. Still, Lynette needs to be told the seriousness of her condition," he kept pressing. "Should I tell her or will you?"

I couldn't believe this man. What was he trying to do? "She knows her condition and I see no need to discuss this with her again. But, if you plan to talk to her about it, I want to be there."

Lynette had finished her class and was waiting for me to wheel her back to her room. I hoped she wouldn't notice how upset I was. Earlier we had told Lynette that the surgeon had removed four new tumors, but was unable to remove the fifth one. We had also told her that her future didn't look too bright, but that nobody knew exactly what was ahead. The pathology report still indicated a non-malignancy, although tests were still being done on the new biopsies. The pathologists were stumped. It appeared to be a new type of tumor.

I knew how disturbed Lynette got whenever we discussed her future. She had a tendency to block out what she didn't want to hear and as a result would become overly optimistic. Who could blame her?

The next day, on February 13th, I arrived early so I could spend the entire day with her. It was her birthday, and I wanted to make it special. Usually she would be watching TV when I came, so when I found her in bed with the covers pulled over her head, I was alarmed.

"Happy birthday, Lynette!"

There was no answer.

"What's the matter, Lynette?"

"The doctor. He wants me to go home to die! Mom, I'm so scared, I don't want to die!" Lynette was almost hysterical. Crying was difficult for her because of her breathing problems, so that she steeled herself whenever she became depressed. Now her shoulders were heaving and I knew she was panicking.

"What else did he say?" I asked as I held her tight.

"He came in and brought another doctor and the head nurse and they all stood around my bed. He told me that my tumor is malignant and I'm going to die within three months. He says I might as well spend the rest of my time at home. Is that true, Mom? Why didn't you tell me?"

"No, Lynette. That is not what Dr. Miller told me. I don't know from where this doctor gets his information. I've asked several doctors who were involved with your surgery and they all say the same thing. It has not been proven to be malignant, but we've been telling you that they couldn't remove all of it. Dr. Miller says you could not live through another surgery like this last one." It seemed cruel but I had to be honest.

"I don't remember what you told me, but I should have known. Everything in life is bad news for me. Whenever I go for a doctor's appointment, it's bad news. Whenever we hope for the easier answer, we get the hard one. Am I going to die in six weeks?"

"O God," I prayed silently, "Help me. How can I tell my own daughter what I don't even want to believe?"

"Lynette, I really don't know. The doctors always answer us with a question, 'How long was it between your surgeries?' That's all the answer we get. Let's figure it out. It was eight months between the last two surgeries, so I'm sure you're going to outlive this doctor's predictions!"

"But I don't want to die. I want to live, get married, and have children. It's not fair to be cheated out of that."

"I know. But who knows when our lives will end. I could die before you do. Life is uncertain for everyone. The important thing is to live so we'll be ready to die anytime. Right now I wish I could take your place." I really meant it. I'd had a good life, and I'd easily have chosen to opt out of mounting trials that I could see on the horizon.

Lynette lay shivering under her blanket.

"Would you like me to pray with you?" I asked.

"Yes, please, but read to me from the Bible first. I need to know that God is helping me." Lynette whispered, "I know that God's will is best for me, but it's so hard to submit to this. It's so hard to believe it's His will for me to die."

I opened the Bible to Romans 8, reading about how sin causes suffering and our body must die, but our spirit lives on if we have been pardoned by Christ. It talked about all of nature groaning for the release of pain and suffering, just like God's children anxiously wait for that day when God will give us full rights, including new bodies that will never again be sick or die. If we don't know exactly how to pray or are too weak to pray the Holy Spirit will pray for us.

"Our heavenly Father knows what the Holy Spirit is saying as he pleads for you in harmony with God's own will."And in verse 28, it says 'We know that all that happens to us is working for our good if we love God and are fitting into His plans.'"

"How can all this be for my good?" Lynette wondered.

"I guess that's where faith and trust come in. If we could understand everything in the Bible, we'd be just as wise as God is, and then we'd all be gods, or God would be merely man. We'll simply have to trust God to work some good out of this."

"Do you really think it's that simple?" Lynette asked with a touch of sarcasm.

"No, Lynette, I didn't mean it would be easy. I know I cannot come close to understanding what you are facing. I, too, have to trust that God will be true to His Word and be the Comforter and Help to you that He has promised. I feel very helpless at a time like this — we both need him! But, listen to verse 35 and on to the end of the chapter:

> Who then can ever keep Christ's love from us? When we have trouble or calamity, when we are hunted down or destroyed, is it because He doesn't love us anymore? And if we are hungry, or penniless, or in danger, or threatened with death, has God deserted us?
>
> No, for the Scriptures tell us that for His sake we must be ready to face death at every moment of the day — we are like sheep awaiting slaughter; but despite all this, overwhelming victory is ours through Christ who loved us enough to die for us.
>
> For I am convinced that nothing can ever separate us from His love. Death can't and life can't. The angels won't, and all the power of hell itself cannot keep God's love away. Our fears for today, our worries about tomorrow, or where we are — high above the sky, or in the deepest ocean — nothing will ever be able to separate us from the love of God demonstrated by our Lord Jesus Christ when He died for us.

"That's speaking right to me, isn't it? Would you read II Corinthians 4:7 to the end of that chapter? Those are some of my favorite verses." Lynette said, much more calmly.

"Certainly!" I found myself feeling quieter too.

But this precious treasure — this light and power that now shine within us — is held in a perishable container, that is, in our weak bodies. Everyone can see that the glorious power within us must be from God and is not our own.

We are pressed on every side by troubles, but not crushed or broken. We are perplexed because we don't know why things happen as they do, but we don't give up and quit. We are hunted down, but God never abandons us. We get knocked down but we get up again and keep going. These bodies of ours are constantly facing death just as Jesus did; so it is clear to all that it is only the living Christ within that keeps us safe.

Yes, we live under constant danger to our lives because we serve the Lord, but this gives us constant opportunities to show forth the power of Jesus Christ within our dying bodies. Because of our preaching we face death, but it has resulted in eternal life for you.

We know that the same God who brought the Lord Jesus back from death will also bring us back to life again with Jesus, and present us to Him along with you. These sufferings of ours are for your benefit. And the more of you who are won to Christ, the more there are to thank Him for his kindness, and the more the Lord is glorified.

That is why we never give up. Though our bodies are dying, our inner strength in the Lord is growing every day. These troubles and sufferings of ours are after all, quite small and won't last very long. Yet this short time of distress will result in God's richest blessing upon us forever and ever. So we do not look at what we can see right now, the troubles all around us, but we look forward to the joys in heaven which we have not yet seen. The troubles will soon be over, but the joys to come will last forever.

Lynette smiled when I finished.

"I guess it's not so bad after all. I'll just finish my struggles here a bit sooner than others my age. I'm so glad I have the hope of going to heaven."

"And I'm so proud of you, Lynette. I'm convinced that your faith is strong enough to see you through. You know, the doctor's talk today has not changed anything in your life. He can't add or subtract one day to your life. It's totally in God's hands. My life could end sooner than yours."

"I know, Mom. I feel much better now. Shall we go have lunch in the cafeteria for my birthday?" she asked, as she sat up grinning.

"Yep, but first I want to give you something special!" I handed her a small gift.

"A birthstone ring! Oh Mom! It's the best present you could have given me. It's beautiful. I love it." I had learned by now to let her do the hugging. A tight squeeze on her shoulders could cause her excruciating pain in her neck.

. . . .

"Happy birthday to you!" our voices rang.

Gathered around the conference table in the nurses' lounge that evening were about 12 or 13 of Lynette's friends and family members. Lynette was bravely attempting her crooked smile as we sang for her. This birthday was one of weirdly mixed emotions, and the party was not as joyful as everyone pretended it to be. After everybody had their fill of cake, jello, ice cream, pop and coffee, there was still over half of everything left.

My sister, Elly, who had prepared all the food for the party, was reluctant to take it back home. "Could you use any of this?" she asked a nurse who happened to pop in.

"Could we ever!" she exclaimed. "Could we use the candles, too? We have another patient who has a birthday today. His family lives in the city right here, but they haven't shown up at all. The staff would love to celebrate with him, if you can spare this."

Elly was only too happy to share the goodies. A few minutes later we watched the young man excitedly blow out the candles on "his" cake, while the nurses and orderlies sang for him. His happy, shining eyes were our ample reward.

After everybody said good-night to Lynette, I was about to leave, too, when she asked me to stay a bit longer. I could see panic mounting in her eyes.

I sat down on the edge of her bed.

"Mom, I'm not going to sleep tonight. I'm scared again. What can I do?"

"Keep your eyes on Jesus, Lynette. Just remember what we read this morning about His love for you. Even your faith is a gift from God. You don't need to do anything but turn to Jesus. He'll help you relax enough to sleep," I said as I held her hand. "Shall we pray together?"

She closed her eyes.

"Dear Lord, thank-you for giving us Lynette these 21 years. She's been such a sweet blessing to us, even during her illness, when she's had to be brave so often. She's had a rough day today and we just want to tell You about it. I ask You to come and take her in Your arms tonight. Help her to relax and put her trust fully in You. Take away her fears and give her a calmness and a restful sleep. In Jesus' name, Amen."

"Thanks, Mom, I'll be OK now. Thanks for everything. Good-night! See you tomorrow!"

Chapter Eighteen

THE ACCIDENT

"I can't believe I'm actually going. Pinch me so I can see if this is real! Pardon me — I probably couldn't feel it anyway!" Lynette said, wryly.

"I could pinch you hard enough to feel it, but I'd probably get arrested for sister abuse when the bruise shows!" Arlene teased.

The girls were off to Kelowna to attend the graduation exercises at OBI. It had been Lynette's dream to return for her classmates' graduation. Although she had to take a wheelchair, she had sufficiently recovered to make the flight, with her sister and cousin Eleanor accompanying her. Her dream was coming true and she was thoroughly enjoying it.

We had cautiously been formulating plans to celebrate our 25th wedding anniversary a week after the girls returned from their trip west. We couldn't go to great lengths, but we felt we owed it to God and our families, as well as our church family, to publicly offer our thanks for everybody's help to us.

On the evening of Saturday, April 27th, our family, friends and relatives gathered in our church basement for worship and praise to God for His goodness to us over the past 25 years. Art and I were truly grateful to be the parents of our four children, one a daughter-in-law. Little Curtis did not appreciate all the attention, so a babysitter took him home.

Cam very ably chaired as emcee, while Janet, Melvin Dueck and Art's brother Jake, led the worship service with selected passages of scripture from the Psalms.

"Bless the Lord, O my soul, and forget not his benefits" was our chosen text. Many an onlooker choked back tears when Arlene softly played "Memories" on the piano, while Lynette, leaning on Cam's arm for support, walked proudly up the platform steps, modelling my original wedding gown. It was Lynette's request to do this, despite the painful looks of pity she knew people would show.

The reception ended romantically when, as a surprise, Art presented me with a bouquet of roses, while a friend sang "The Rose" to Arlene's piano accompaniment.

Janet was in her glory later as she helped us unwrap the many gifts. Nothing could excite her more than opening a wrapped box. She could hardly contain herself that night. Watching her was like seeing a kid on Christmas Eve!

As I hugged her afterward, I told her how much I appreciated her.

"You know, Janet, I love you just like one of my own daughters. You've helped make tonight complete and I want to thank you for it."

Nothing could be truer. Janet had done a lot of "behind-the-scenes" work, making and mounting decorations. She had done it all happily, adding the touch of excitement that the rest of us had been lacking.

The unusually warm April weather had dried the fields, so that seeding was early and most of the wheat was in by the first weekend in May. As a treat, Art and I allowed ourselves the luxury during a busy season to spend a night in a Winnipeg hotel on school trustee business. Lynette spent the evening at Cam and Janet's house while Arlene participated in a drama at school, after which the kids went to the city for a late supper.

When we got home the next day we found Arlene in a state of extreme agitation.

"What happened now?" Art asked.

"Dad, please don't be mad!"

"What happened?" his voice was rising.

"I had an accident last night." Arlene said quietly.

"How bad? Who got hurt?" I was relieved that Arlene was all right, but she looked so worried. . . .

"Nobody. Nobody got hurt, but the car is pretty bad." She began to cry, "I'm sorry . . . it was my fault."

She explained how she had tried to keep up with a friend's car because she hadn't known her way out of the city. In turning a corner, she switched lanes too quickly and was hit by a taxi. Our car was totalled!

All weekend Arlene was plagued by the guilty thought that she had added to the problems of the Cornelsen household. She also began to wonder what would have happened to her, had she been killed in the accident. On Monday evening, a friend picked her up, and together they went to visit a neighboring couple, the church youth group leaders. I was still up when Arlene came home.

"Mom, I did it tonight. I gave my life over to God. I've been very angry and bitter about Lynette's illness and all these things that have happened to our family, but tonight Bob and Dorothy showed me how God could help me handle these feelings. I finally have peace about it, but I'll need lots of prayers yet."

I squeezed her and breathed a "Praise the Lord!"

As she made her way downstairs to her bedroom, she called back, "Don't forget to pick me up at school for our appointment at the police station tomorrow afternoon." The business of reporting her accident in the city had not yet been taken care of.

The next morning dawned bright and clear. Art and Cam prepared for another day of seeding while I got Arlene off to school and Lynette dressed for the day. The phone rang. It was a message for Art, so I called the farm and Janet answered.

"Sure, I'll tell Dad," she said cheerfully.

"Thanks. What are you doing today? Are you going to Kim's baby shower this afternoon?" I asked.

"Oh yes, I wouldn't miss that, but I have to go to the city this morning to shop for a few things. My Mom and Dad are coming out for my brother's wedding next weekend, and Cam says I can buy myself some new clothes!" Janet sounded excited.

"Good for you! What are you doing with Curtis?"

"Oh, I can take him along. He loves the ride!"

"Well, have a good day. See you later."

"Bye."

After lunch, Lynette and I drove over to the Rempels' house for my niece's shower. Kim was surprised that Janet hadn't shown up yet, but I assured her she'd be there soon.

"You know Janet, she'll come breezing in any minute now," I said.

But she didn't.

I had to pick up Arlene at 4:00 p.m., so Lynette and I left the shower. I accompanied Arlene into the police station and helped her fill out her accident report.

The clerk asked me to sign my name and then asked, "You are Mrs. Art Cornelsen, right?"

I nodded. She took the signed paper over to the desk and came back.

"Would you two step into the office, please?" she asked. Arlene looked at me and whispered, "Is the cop going to lecture me now?"

"You'd probably deserve it, wouldn't you?" I answered heartlessly.

The police officer who entered the office was very friendly, however.

"Is Art your husband?" he asked me.

"Yes.

"And Cam is your son?"

"Yes." What did these questions have to do with Arlene's accident?

"I'm afraid I have bad news for you. There's been an accident."

Art? Cam? Who? Why doesn't he go on?

"Your daughter-in-law was in the city?"

"Yes!"

"Her car was hit by a grain truck. She didn't make it to the hospital."

"No! No! NO!" I heard someone screaming. It was Arlene.

"I'm sorry," the officer said.

"What about the little boy? She had Curtis with her," I asked.

"He's fine. He's waiting to be picked up at Victoria Hospital."

Arlene was wailing. "You mean Janet's dead? I can't take it. God hates us. Why does He do this to us?"

"Arlene, I don't know why. We have to trust God to help us now. He's helped us before. He'll do it again. He has to! He has to!" I was not as calm as I tried to appear.

What a nightmare! "O Lord, may I wake up soon?"

The officer was speaking again.

"Shall I drive you home?"

"No, I'd better hurry home to tell Cam. He and Art are on the field. Nobody will be able to find them."

We hurried out. The look of utterly helpless compassion on the officer's face matched the genuine pain in his voice as he repeated the words, "I'm so sorry."

Arlene's loud cries alarmed Lynette, who was waiting for us in the car.

"What's happened to her?" Lynette asked me.

Lynette and Janet had been exceptionally close as sisters-in-law. When I broke the painful news to Lynette, she began to weep silently. I prayed for a clear head for the drive home, but Arlene continued to wail loudly. In desperation, I began to sing, however shakily:

> Turn your eyes upon Jesus,
> Look full in His wonderful face
> And the things of earth will grow strange-
> ly dim
> In the light of His glory and grace.

It seemed to take forever to drive the ten miles home. Jake and Joyce Cornelsen were waiting for us at our house. Everybody in Rosenort knew about the accident already — we'd been the last to hear, it seemed.

Somebody had located the men on the field. Our pastor had gone to inform them and bring them home. Numbly I went out to meet them as they drove onto the yard. Art got out of the car first. When Cam followed, he crumpled to the ground. I sat down beside him and just held him. Silently, he got up, walked into the house and phoned Janet's brother, who lived 30 miles away. He moved around mechanically, saying little. Our pastor offered to drive us to the city to pick up Curtis.

Seeing Curtis playing with toys in the nurses' lounge broke the spell somewhat. There was a dark bruise on his forehead and strap burns on his arms, but otherwise he was in fine shape. My mother heart was breaking again. . . .

"O Lord, when will the pain stop? Why must this innocent little 18-month-old boy be motherless? Why must my young married son lose his beautiful wife? O, God, help us!"

Our house quickly filled with sympathetic friends. It was late before I was able to help Lynette prepare for the night. I found her lying on the bed, wide-eyed and shaking.

"Are you going to be all right?" I asked.

"I don't know, Mom. I just can't believe Janet's really gone. Remember you told me anyone could die sooner than me? It actually happened!"

"God works in strange ways, doesn't He?"

"I wonder what it's like to die. I wonder what Janet felt. You know, Mom, when I think of it, it'll be easier for me to go now. I'll have a sister waiting to show me around heaven. Is that dumb?" Lynette asked, her eyes shining with brimming tears.

"No, Lynette. That's not dumb. I can just picture Janet, hand in hand with Jesus, waiting for you. It's going to be hard for the rest of us, now, but we'll all be coming to join you eventually," I said as I gripped her hand.

Lynette relaxed.

I was talking more bravely than I felt. Inwardly I sent up my SOS. "O, Lord help us all!" Once again, God undertook and carried us through.

The days before the funeral became a blur of people, more people, food, flowers, and funeral arrangements. Cam and Curtis slept together on our living room floor. One night, I had put Curtis to sleep in his playpen in Art's office. I was only half-awake when I thought I heard a baby crying. Somewhere out there in the dark was a baby crying, and I was supposed to be responsible for a baby, my monitor was telling me.

"That's dumb, I don't have a baby."

The sound was persistent. I got up and walked in the direction it was coming from. Fearfully, I reached into the darkness. Slowly I began to wake up and the terrors of the true situation hit me full force. The baby was still crying.

'Pick him up before everybody wakes up,' my monitor instructed.

"Mommy, Mommy. . . ."

Curtis looked up at me with fear on his face and screamed louder.

By now Cam was up and took Curtis out of my arms. I prepared juice in his bottle, and he quieted down as Cam snuggled him under his blanket beside him. The tyke fell asleep, but Cam asked me to stay and talk.

"Mom, what will I do? I can't look after Curtis full-time. Even if I had the time, I'm not a mother. I can't look after him. I don't know how. Should I look for somebody who can take him in?"

"Do you have somebody in mind?"

"Yes. In fact, one of Janet's friends has offered to take him."

"Is it what you want, Cam?"

"No, of course not. I know he would be well taken care of and loved, but I can't just give my little boy away. I love him. I need him myself. Is that selfish?"

"Will you give me a chance to look after him? Dad and I want you both to move in with us. Would you consider it?"

"You've got your hands full, Mom. I can't add another burden to what you already have. You have more than you can handle now."

"Let me try, OK?"

"All right, but we'll have to hire some help for you. Thanks, Mom. You and Dad are so good to me. I couldn't handle this without you. It's so unbelievable!" We talked quietly for several hours before Cam was ready to settle down again.

Janet's parents, sister, grandmother, aunts and uncles from various parts of Canada, who had planned to come for her brother's wedding, now came a week earlier to attend the funeral as well.

The day of the funeral was cold, wet and blustery, but the service was one of joy and victory. On arrival at the church, we were amazed to see the viewing lineup filling the entire length of the sidewalk beside the church. Janet, who had been a complete stranger in our community only four years ago, now drew a crowd of 700 friends to her memorial service, including her doctor from the city, the young man who had driven the truck into her path, and the policeman who had attended the accident.

Everybody in our church was deeply touched by Janet's sudden passing. Having always been friendly and vivacious, sweet Janet was now sadly missed, especially by the young couples. They showed their love by reaching out to Cam in many beautiful ways, often inviting him for coffee and listening to him unload his grief.

A prayer we found in one of the cards sent to us truly expressed our feelings:

> Lord God, in the shock of the moment, I do not understand; I do not know; I cannot comprehend what has happened. Help me to really believe that you know and that you are able to sustain me now and always. Amen.

Art and I would add a few lines of our own prayer "And, Lord, while you're holding us up, please give us more time with Lynette — we can't give her up just yet. Another six months at least. Please?"

Chapter Nineteen

COPING

"How are you doing?"

"OK."

"Are you sure you're all right?"

"No, but we're coping."

The summer months following Janet's death remain a blur in my mind, although certain incidents stand out vividly.

Curtis was a very demanding child. I began to understand Janet's frequent weariness, backaches, and late mornings. How had she managed to paper and paint walls, strip and varnish old furniture, and have time to have coffee with friends? It took all my time just keeping Curtis diapered, fed and happy. Hour after hour of rocking made a slave out of Grandma.

My mornings usually began around seven, when Curtis awoke. Originally, we had planned for Curtis to sleep in Cam's room, but we quickly realized that they kept each other awake and neither one was getting enough sleep, so we moved the crib into the extra bedroom. It was next door to Lynette, allowing me to look after both of them more easily.

I began my new routine by making breakfast for Art, Cam, and Curtis; Arlene would manage to get off to school by herself. Usually, Curtis would have a messy diaper before I got him dressed, so he'd get a bath, which was his highlight. By then Lynette would be awake and asking for breakfast. I'd take her a tray of cereal, milk and toast, and quickly dry and dress Curtis while she ate. Afterwards, I'd help Lynette onto a chair in the bathtub, where she could manage to turn on the shower by herself. Leaving her busy there, I'd go make her bed, while Curtis rolled around with pillows on the floor or pulled the sheets to tease me.

"O Curtis, if you weren't so adorable, I'd . . ."

"Of course, I'd never give you away. You are my own flesh and blood. I love you. I NEED you."

That was it. I needed the playfulness, the happiness of this child to break the depressing atmosphere in our home.

After her bath, Lynette would need help with dressing, as well as putting in her contact lenses and earrings. Then she'd spend a half-hour on her own, having devotions before moving into the living room. On good days she could walk by herself; on other days I'd have to assist her. When it was warm and sunny, I'd help her outside where she loved to lie on her lounge in the sunshine. By taking Curtis out too, I was able to keep an eye on them both.

By 11:30 I often felt more like going to bed than making lunch. It was a challenge trying to keep Curtis awake until dishes were cleaned up. To start the afternoon, I'd help Lynette to her room and turn on her TV set. Then I'd grab a bottle of juice and sing and rock Curtis to sleep. During the lull someone frequently dropped by for a cup of coffee and an encouraging chat. By 3:00 Lynette and Curtis would both want attention. I'd settle them in the living room, where Lynette did a great job of playing with her little nephew. The bond between them was strong. Curtis sensed that Lynette was the only one who had extra time for him!

Supper time was unpredictable. Having missed his daddy during the day, supper was Curtis's opportunity to demand attention. On his good days Cam was able to keep Curtis happy by talking to him, but our son had many days when he longed desperately for Janet, and Curtis's large, brown eyes simply reminded him of her. Grief would well up in him and rob his appetite entirely. Such affected Lynette too: she would be very quiet and stay in her room more. Art's time was taken up almost totally with consoling Cam: talking to him, often just being with him.

Our plight seemed bleak to the point of being futile: Janet was gone and the farm empty; the rest of us huddled together in pain and perplexity — Cam grieving deeply, Curtis needing mothering, Lynette living on borrowed time and also needing help and attending, and Arlene struggling with spiritual uncertainty and teenage peer pressures in the midst of these trying circumstances. Art and I were pushed near the edge of despair. Questions about the point in living punctuated our struggle:

Would we ever be a normal family again?

What was normal?

When would the pain stop?

Did God really understand our heartache in seeing our children hurt so much?

One day a niece in Calgary called me. She had attended OBC with Lynette and was very concerned about her cousin's health.

"Hi, how are you doing?" Bev asked.

"OK. We're busy. Don't have time to figure out how we're doing," I answered.

"Can I do anything to help?"

"Bev, we're praying for help around the house. You wouldn't happen to want to change jobs for a while, would you?" I asked carefully.

"I could manage that."

"You don't understand. We need someone to do dishes, make meals, wash floors, babysit, keep Lynette company — be my right-hand assistant."

"I'd like to come."

"Think you could handle Lynette's illness and handicaps?" I asked.

"I'll try."

"How soon can you come?"

"Next week OK?"

"Bless you, Bev."

And so God sent us Bev. She made it possible for me to get out of the house occasionally. She helped Lynette through long, lonely hours when I simply did not have time for her. She looked after Curtis when I had to take Lynette for appointments or just out for a Coke.

To Arlene, Bev became the sisterly confidante that Lynette was becoming less of. Not only was Bev a Godsend to our household, but to my widowed mother she became a very welcome companion when she spent her evenings and nights with her.

Arlene had taken a summer job at the local coffee shop. Outwardly, she seemed to have accepted Janet's death, but she was still struggling to comprehend why God had allowed it to happen. She had just begun to accept Lynette's illness when the accident occurred. Watching her sister literally drag herself around the house and hearing Cam weep night after night, were taking their toll on Arlene. She tried to be away as often as possible, attempting to escape the harsh realities at home. I couldn't blame her, but I prayed that she would find comfort from the right sources.

Having lived with Lynette's illness had helped us accept her death as inevitable, but none of us was prepared for the sudden loss of our lively, effervescent daughter-in-law. In the previous three years, moreover, we had lost my father, Art's mother, and an 18-month-old grandniece. Within a month of Janet's accident, three more members of our church passed away. It was almost more than we could cope with, and for a while a pall seemed to hang over the entire community.

Melvin and Anne Dueck would drop in occasionally to lift our spirits. We never ceased to marvel at Melvin's cheerfulness, but it became increasingly evident that his health was failing rapidly and that he lived in constant pain. His doctors had told him there was no cure for his liver disease; they could only hope to keep him somewhat comfortable with Prednisone and pain killers. Whenever we could get away, Art and I would join them for miniature golf, a cup of coffee, or just a ride, but always to talk. We spent many an hour chatting about trivial things, but more often sharing our hurts and praying together. Without verbalizing it, we sensed that our good times together were coming to an end.

People continued to ask me how I coped with the enormous amount of stress.

"You're taking it so well," they would say.

I began to wonder if I wasn't capable of grieving "properly." How could I explain the deep pain that I couldn't express in words? Or the utter exhaustion from looking after Curtis and Lynette, which prevented me from thinking? Or those times when I resented the busyness that kept me from indulging in "proper grief"? Or the guilt feelings from going out some evenings, trying to escape my responsibilities at home? Or the trapped feeling when I came back to find it all waiting for me again?

Grief is strange to live with. It found its expression in many ways, ways so varied that I didn't always identify it as such. At times there was only numbness. At other times, I would feel betrayed. Emotions of hostility, resentment, fear and guilt, all threatened to tear my insides apart. In trying to keep a degree of normalcy in the household, however, I could not afford the luxury of giving in to my feelings.

"But you have to unburden yourself, or you'll get sick," I'd be advised. The only answer I could give was, "Please let me know when I am sick I might not notice!"

Art and I had always treasured bedtime as our opportunity to hold forth on the day's happenings, share problems, and victories, and have devotions and prayer together. Now even that refuge was gone. Art usually spent an hour or two with Cam in the evening, while I prepared Lynette for bed. After she was settled, I'd rock Curtis to sleep; Art and Cam, meanwhile, would retire for the night. Before I'd lie down I'd check on Lynette. If she was sleeping, I'd quickly climb into my bed, where Art was likely to be snoring. Almost without fail, at midnight a tiny voice would begin to cry, "Mommy." If I got him his bottle immediately, he would sometimes go back to sleep without rocking. If he woke Lynette, it would mean massaging her sore neck muscles before she could go back to sleep.

A well-meaning friend frequently said "I'm so glad you have little Curtis. He'll help you get over your grief."

In essence this was true, but I struggled with resentment over such a remark. How could I tell her that little Curtis kept me from grieving like I wanted to? There were times when I just longed to crawl into my bed and weep myself to sleep.

Sometimes, when I was rocking Curtis, I'd study his face, wondering what was going on in his little mind: whether he remembered his mother, whether he'd ever have another mother, what the future would hold for him.

So often he would put his tiny arms around my neck and with a big bear hug say, "I love you, Mommy." He had very naturally accepted me as his mother, trusting me completely to meet his needs. He was such a sweet child, filling my life with so much love and happiness.

Yes, Curtis was helping me to cope with Lynette's illness, but did God have to use such drastic measures? No, I didn't believe He took Janet for that reason. He could have helped me in an easier way.

The "whys" kept returning without answers.

"The Lord will have to answer a lot of questions some day when I see Him," I said bitterly one day.

"When you see the Lord, your questions will all be answered," my sister responded gently.

"That's true!" I thought. "O Lord, I can hardly wait to see you. I know you have a purpose for me in all this turmoil. Just give me the strength and patience I need to continue. Thanks for the opportunity to serve You, but help me!"

I picked up a pen and wrote the following lines:

> When I cry, "Why me?"
> The Lord answers, "Why not you?"
> "But I don't understand," I complain.

"You don't have to," He replies, "Trust me. My Son suffered too. I understand."

"I'm so tired and weak. I can't take any more."

"That's all right. When you're weak I'll give you my strength."

"I'm afraid. It's dark. I can't see ahead."

"Just keep your eyes on me. I am The Way."

"But I feel so alone."

"I will never leave you. I love you and I want what is best for you. The way may seem hard, rough and sometimes impossible to walk. That is when my strong arms pick you up and carry you. Someday you will see that this is your way to glorify me."

During my bout with cancer, when Psalm 116 had become so important to me, several verses seemed to be telling me to repay God by serving Him in a special way. I was overwhelmed with gratitude for His deliverance and wanted to tell everyone that God heals. I promised to offer God a "sacrifice of thanksgiving" by giving my testimony whenever the opportunity arose.

I had written out my story and waited for the opportunity to present it. Finally, when I was asked to speak at our church ladies' group, I eagerly agreed. A friend encouraged me to prepare a talk for the Christian Women's Club. That was all the encouragement I needed. I knew, however, that one didn't just volunteer to speak, the Club had to extend an invitation.

"Lord, if You want me to speak, I'm willing to wait for the right timing. I'm not going to run ahead of You. If You want me to praise You publicly for healing me, then You will have to make the arrangements."

A year went by during which several ladies in the community had mastectomies but were not as fortunate as I had been. They all had to undergo painful therapies; two of them died within months. The others recuperated but had a very difficult time readjusting.

I feared how my testimony might affect these women or their families. I could well imagine how self-righteous and insensitive I would appear. My bout with cancer seemed insignificant beside theirs. It did not make me less grateful toward God but more sensitive to the feelings of those less fortunate than I had been.

It was then that Lynette got sick, however, and I forgot about further speaking engagements. Another year went by, during which Lynette had another surgery and rallied somewhat.

Then the invitations came.

"O Lord, do You really expect me to speak in the midst of my pain? My story isn't complete yet. Let me wait until the storm is past. There is too much confusion right now."

I could almost here God answer, "Are you going back on your promise? Haven't I helped you this far? Do you think I can't help you speak? Besides, if you don't do it in My strength, it's useless anyway. I want you to do it in your weakness, in My strength, now."

Several invitations came for me to speak that winter, which I had to decline because Lynette had just had her third surgery that January. However, I accepted two invitations for the spring. I spoke once in April, and a second engagement was scheduled for June in the neighboring town of Morris. My friends, who knew of the commitment, wondered how I'd be able to talk publicly about Lynette's illness. I myself wasn't sure whether I could manage it, especially since Lynette, Janet and Arlene were also looking forward to attending the meeting.

And then Janet had her fatal accident! I was scheduled to speak three weeks later. Could I do it? As the time drew near, there was no question in my mind. I knew the Lord would provide me with the strength I needed; but I did not expect Him to give me joy as well.

As I watched the hall fill up with ladies, I realized that most of them were my personal friends. People kept coming in until every place was filled. Extra tables and chairs set out were filled as well. The loving support I felt was overwhelming, and I could hardly wait to proclaim what a wonderful God and loving Heavenly Father we have, and what He had done for me. As I experienced the exhilarating feeling of being carried in God's strong arms, I prayed that the Holy Spirit would minister powerfully to the hearts of the women there. Not once did I feel like weeping; I was surprised to see tears in the audience.

Since then I've had numerous opportunities to speak. To relate with greater sensitivity to those who have known the depths of suffering, however, I needed to go through deeper waters. Our trials were not yet over. I would need the grace of God to see me through the rest of that summer.

Chapter Twenty

FAMILY FUN

One day in June, Dr. Miller called our home and asked to speak to Art. He had received the results of Lynette's latest CAT scan and asked for Art and me to come in the next day.

"Just Rose and me?" Art asked in surprise.

"Yes. It might be better for Lynette not to come this time. It's not good news!" Dr. Miller's voice was compassionate. In the office the next day, Dr. Miller showed us the X-rays. He shook his head sadly.

"There are new tumor satellites springing up all over. There are several on the left side now, as well as on the right. The tumor that we didn't touch in her last surgery has grown too. I'm sorry, but I don't think there's any more we can do for her."

"Is there no place in the States or Europe or anywhere that they'd be better equipped for this kind of brain surgery?" I asked, grasping at straws.

"No, I'm sorry, we've checked all over. If we could prove it was malignant we would give her chemotherapy, but it still doesn't test that way. She's had the maximum dosage of cobalt, so that's out. Surgery is definitely out of the question. She's had enough torture."

"How much time does she have left?"

"I really can't say. It depends on how fast the tumors grow. It could be that she is in immediate danger."

"You mean, she could go fast?" I was alarmed.

"It's quite possible, yes." Dr. Miller wasn't sparing us this time at all, but we could see the pain in his eyes.

"Thanks for telling us. I guess it is better to know exactly what the situation is, but I'm not sure just what we'll tell Lynette. She'll want to know what you said."

What a merry-go-round! Just when we were adjusting to a certain way of life, we had to cope with a new shock.

"Well? What's the bad news now? When am I going to die?" Lynette asked with a wry grin when we came home. She often made it easier for us by making forthright remarks like this.

"Don't sound so hopeful!" I tried to sound cheerful when actually my stomach felt sick with dread. What was I supposed to say?

"Lord, help me again," I pleaded silently.

"Can't you tell me either? I know why Dr. Miller didn't need to see me. It must have been bad news again."

"You're right, it wasn't very good. It looks like that one tumor is growing again. He said chemotherapy might be the answer."

"I knew it. But I'm going to fight it. I don't think I want chemotherapy though. I wouldn't want to be bald at my own funeral!" Lynette sounded flippant, but I caught the note of hopelessness in her voice. I put my arm around her gently.

"Remember, Lynette, nothing has really changed. We didn't receive good news today, but you are no sicker today than yesterday. God is still the same and we're still trusting Him to help us. We're all in this together, OK?"

"Sure," Lynette said, as she got up to go to her room.

She and I both knew that what I said had a hollow ring to it. Of course, we would help her all that we could; she knew that. But, ultimately, only she would walk the lonely road leading to her grave. Nobody could do that for her.

"How would you like to go to the lake for the weekend, Lynette," Art asked at supper time one day.

"Me and who else?"

"Yeah, what about me?" Arlene wanted to know.

"And me and Curtis?" Cam asked.

"Sure, why don't we all go? Bev could come, too."

"How can we? Our camper can't hold us all, and it would be too cool at night, and we'd need a bathroom for Lynette and Curtis. There would be that step to climb — impossible with a wheelchair. . . ." I was thinking of how much work it was to look after the two at home, never mind camping. I'd rather stay home.

"No, no, we'll get a motel room for you girls. I'll drive you down in the car and Cam can bring the pickup. Cam and I can sleep on the back of the pickup — we'll put on the camper shell." Art's optimistic enthusiasm was catching, and the family began to plan.

Ordinarily a camping weekend would have been organized fairly quickly, but this would take a little more thought.

"I hope you remembered everything," Art said with a grin as he closed the loaded camper shell.

"So do I. I can't believe all this stuff! Bottles, diapers, wheelchair, stroller, playpen, medication, barbecue, lawn chairs, even the rocking chair!"

"Come on, Curtis, climb in. We're going to the lake!"

Away we went, Arlene and Curtis in the truck with Cam, Lynette and Bev in the car with Art and me. Everyone was in great spirits. We were going to leave our cares behind and for one short weekend pretend that everything was just fine.

The weekend was a highlight for us that summer. My sister and brother-in-law, Elly and Johnny, and their daughter, Pam, accompanied us. It was good to watch the teenagers acting like teenagers and yet adjusting their pace to accommodate Lynette in her wheelchair. It was so much fun that we decided to spend another weekend at a large hotel in Winnipeg a month later. This time our family went alone.

Going up to our room on the 19th floor at the downtown Holiday Inn, we had to hang on to Curtis, who thought he needed to get off the elevator every time it stopped. Once we were in our room, he began to explore. Art went out onto the balcony and lifted Curtis up so he could look over the railing.

"Froe down," Curtis yelled gleefully, propelling his running shoe high into the air. We watched it land below us on another part of the hotel. It was quite a challenge for Art to make his way out onto the roof to retrieve it!

"Let's go swimming in the pool," Lynette suggested eagerly.

"You? Go swimming?" I asked incredulously.

"Why not?"

"If you go swimming, you're not my responsibility," I said heartlessly. "If your Dad and Cam look after you, you can go, I guess," relenting a little.

It was Lynette's first time in a pool since her last surgery.

She didn't attempt to swim, but walked along the buoy rope in the water. She tired quickly, so she and I sat in the whirlpool watching the others dive and swim. Curtis was soon ready to get dressed, and Art offered to take him back to the room. Cam and Arlene had to dress for their dates, leaving Lynette and me to enjoy the hot pool just a bit longer.

"Oh-h-h, this feels so-o-o good! Oh, what's that, a fire alarm?" Lynette asked me.

It was indeed a fire alarm and folks were leaving the swimming pool, which was on the third floor.

"Let's ignore it," I suggested. "It's probably a false alarm. Besides, if it's for real, we'll likely get stuck somewhere with the wheelchair."

The pool attendant noticed us just sitting there.

"I'm sorry, you'll have to leave the pool area," she told us.

"But my daughter has to go in a wheelchair. . . ." I tried to explain.

"You can't stay here, you have to get out of the building quickly!"

We did our best. Wrapping a towel around Lynette and grabbing mine as well, I helped her to the wheelchair. Upon reaching the elevators, I wasn't surprised to find that they weren't in operation. Now what? The stairs? Lynette could walk stairs with assistance, but she'd need the wheelchair outside.

A couple came running down the hall, heading for the fire exit. Seeing our dilemma, they stopped and offered to help us.

"Oh, would you please? If you could bring the wheelchair, I can help her walk."

The four of us went thumping down three flights of stairs. Upon reaching the exit, the door opened to reveal pouring rain.

"You want to go out there?" they asked us.

"No way. Lynette's getting too chilled already. Let's try the door on second floor," I suggested.

Back up two flights, Lynette was visibly tired but kept on moving like a trooper. The couple, like guardian angels, dragged the wheelchair between the two of them.

We finally reached a door that opened to the mezzanine floor. We could see the goings-on from the balcony. Hundreds of people stood around in the lobby watching a dozen or so firemen running back and forth. While we stood there, I thanked the couple for their help.

"You're quite welcome. We were glad to help. Do you mind telling us about your daughter, why she's in a wheelchair?" the friendly stranger asked.

We talked a while, and he informed us that he had retired from his job after having had a heart attack. Careless of his own danger, however, he had willingly dragged the wheelchair up and down the stairs for us. We were grateful.

After about 15 minutes the panic was over. False alarm! We hurried up the elevator to our room and found Art and Curtis calmly watching TV. They hadn't bothered to heed the fire alarm at all. Thank God there was no actual danger. Nonetheless swimming was off the agenda for Lynette and me for the rest of the weekend.

Back at home while preparing for bed on Sunday night, Lynette heaved a big sigh.

"Well, Lynette, what do you think, was it all worth the effort?" I asked as I massaged her neck.

"Oh, yes, Mom, it was fun wasn't it? Imagine seeing you standing on the Mezzanine floor at Holiday Inn in your wet bathing suit?" she giggled as she eased back onto her pillow carefully. She turned serious and said earnestly, "Thanks so much, Mom. I know it's not easy for you, but it's so good to get out. We have a great family, don't we?"

Chapter Twenty-one

SEEKING HEALING

"Mom, when did you say Mr. Reed was going to be in the city?" Lynette asked me one morning in August.

"You mean the faith healer?"

"Yes. Do you think we could go?" she asked cautiously.

"Is that what you want?" I asked. I had seen an ad in the city paper and mentioned it rather casually. We had never fully discussed the subject of seeking out a faith healer. Our own church ministers had prayed over her and anointed her with oil on several occasions. We believed we had followed Biblical teaching and trusted God to honor our prayers, even if He wasn't answering according to our wishes.

"I'd very much like to go," Lynette answered quietly.

"Are you prepared to handle it if he turns out to be a charlatan?" I did not want her to build up false hopes. "I've never heard of this man before. What if he's one of those who makes money a big issue or plays heavily on your emotions? I don't want you upset," I warned.

"I believe God can protect me from anything evil. I have to give it a try. Please?" Lynette didn't beg very often, but when she did, I was putty in her hands.

"OK. Let's ask some friends to go with us. Arlene has to work, and your Dad and Cam are preparing for harvest. Whom shall we ask?"

We took Lynette's Aunt Nita, Aunt Evelyn and her daughter, Eleanor. Before getting out of the car at the meeting, I suggested, "Why don't we have prayer before we go in? I'm concerned that we don't fall into the evil one's hands tonight. Let's pray for healing, of course, but only according to God's plan and timing."

131

I realized how nervous Lynette was when I saw her trembling fingers. She longed for a dramatic healing.

We were ushered into a fairly small meeting room, with seating for about 70. People straggled in until the place was about half full. It seemed a long wait before an obese man, weighing all of 350 pounds, made his way up the aisle. He led the group in singing beautiful songs of worship, dispelling my niggling doubts. Surely such a worshipful service could not be based on false teachings. Lynette smiled at me as she began to relax.

After an hour of singing, a second man entered the room. Tall, slender, and flashily dressed, we sensed this was the man we were waiting for. The audience hushed as he approached the pulpit.

"Good evening! It's good to see you at our first meeting. We're in for a great time together with the Lord. I'm sure the Lord will meet your needs tonight. You have come for healing and you will not be disappointed. You will be healed tonight!"

His voice rose in volume and the people clapped.

"To begin the meeting, we will have a love offering. Let us show the Lord how much we love Him by our giving. . . ." He expounded the virtues and blessings of giving generously. The audience was asked to go up and deposit their gifts of money into the basket that the speaker was holding.

All my defenses went up. I refused to buy God's favor. I did not believe He worked that way. Surely, if this was a man of God, it wouldn't matter to him whether I contributed to the offering. I didn't move.

After the offering, the minister began to speak, "the Word of the Lord" and prophesy. He moved from person to person, praying over each one. We sat near the back, Lynette in the aisle with her wheelchair. As the speaker drew nearer, he passed right by Lynette to get to me and my sister.

"You live in great fear of what your future holds, but God tells you not to fear; He will strengthen you, He will help you, yea, He will uphold you with the right hand of righteousness."

He was quoting directly from Isaiah 41:10, a verse my high school principal had given me at my graduation. Coincidence? Maybe not!

I was dismayed, however, when he walked right past Lynette a second time, ignoring her. Why didn't he pray over her? Sitting in a wheelchair, it was very obvious that she was the one who had come for help.

Upon finishing the prophesies, Mr. Reed returned to the pulpit. Looking directly at me, he announced a second offering. This time the money was to go for rental of the meeting room.

I reasoned I would give him all the money I had after he had prayed over Lynette. Until then, I had no desire to put any money into this man's hands. I was still not assured of his genuineness and his motives.

By the time he began to preach, it was 9:30 p.m. His theme was the love of God for the world. God sacrificed His own son, Jesus, to pay for the sins of the world, so that believing in Him, we could be saved. His words drew vivid pictures in my mind, and my heart overflowed with gratitude to God for His great gift of love. Surely, this speaker spoke words of truth! An hour later, he finally ended the message.

"We will be having a healing service in just a few minutes, but first we must have another offering. This money will go for my wages. I need a large amount of money to pay for my travelling expenses, as well as my living. This is my only source of income. The Lord has told me there are ten people here who want to pay $100 each. Will those ten please raise their hands? One? Two? Any more? All right, are there ten people who will give $50 each? Three? Thank-you. How many of you will give $25? One, two, three, five? Anyone else?"

I was getting angry. How dare a purported man of God so destroy the beautiful atmosphere that a moment before appeared to have been Spirit-filled? I glanced at Lynette.

"Do you want to leave?" I asked her.

She shook her head.

Mr. Reed went on.

"All right. We'll go on with the healing service. All you who want healing, please come forward. As you come, you may enclose your offering in the envelopes that are placed on the floor here at the front."

"Do you want to go, Lynette?" I whispered.

She nodded.

"Do you want me to give an offering?" I asked her.

She shook her head.

I pushed the wheelchair and parked her squarely in front of Mr. Reed. He could not ignore her now.

"Haven't we met before?" he asked.

"No, I don't think so," Lynette replied.

"I have met you in the spirit, I'm sure," said Mr. Reed. "Would you please move to the end of the line?" he added. I was furious! It was almost 11:00 p.m., and Lynette was so tired she could hardly sit up. There were dozens of people who had come up behind us, yet we were asked to move to the end. What kind of a game was this?

"Are you sure you want to stay?" I asked again.

Lynette nodded again.

As we stood waiting, we watched Mr. Reed cup his hand under the people's chins to pray over them. As he prayed, each person would fall over backward, where the songleader stood ready to catch him. I had attended a service like this before, but Lynette was terrified as she saw dozens of people fall to the floor, apparently unconscious. One pregnant lady began to cry as the man prayed. She had not received the "slaying in the Spirit" as she had hoped.

Mr. Reed stepped up to face the audience and spoke authoritatively. "Listen everybody, I'm going to ask you to do something special. Don't ask any questions. Just do as I say. I want everybody to come up here and give me one dollar. Not $2 or $5. Just one dollar each . . . come up here. . . ."

I looked at Lynette. She was shaking uncontrollably.

"Let's go home," she said.

I did not hesitate. Somehow we were able to push our way out, zigzagging past people in various stages of consciousness on the floor.

." . . and give your money to this lady," the speaker was still instructing as we left.

Once out the door, we began to laugh hysterically. We all remained disturbed, however. I could hardly forgive myself for having exposed Lynette to this charlatan. Her depth of shock and disappointment evidenced itself in a tearful, sleepless night.

Why did her hopes always have to be dashed?

Alvin and Adina Kornelsen, deacons from our church, frequently dropped in to visit Lynette and pray with her. They came the day after we'd been to the healing service. As we related the events of the day before, we found that we were able to laugh.

"Have you ever considered going to see Dr. John White?"

"You mean the Christian psychiatrist?" I asked.

"Yes, but he's not practicing as a medical doctor anymore. He is mostly writing books and lecturing now, but God has given him the gift of healing and many people have been wonderfully and supernaturally healed through his prayers."

"Sounds great, but I'm not sure Lynette could handle another emotional upset. What do you think, Lynette?"

"Oh yeah, I'd go right away, but where is he? In the city? Or on the other side of the world somewhere?"

"He travels all over the world, but the reason I thought of him now is because I've seen him every day this week. He's over at Winnipeg Bible College, teaching a summer course for two weeks. Maybe he'd have time to see you. Want me to try and get you an appointment?" Alvin asked.

"Please do," Lynette whispered eagerly.

"O Lord, please don't let her down," I prayed silently.

Two days later my sister Elly and I helped Lynette up the steps at WBC. We were met at the door by Alvin and Adina and a man we had never met before. He had the kindest eyes and softest voice I had ever heard. His compassion for Lynette was so obvious that my eyes blurred. I immediately sensed we were experiencing God's love through this quiet, humble, gray-haired man. He led us to his study.

"You have come for physical healing, Lynette?"

She nodded.

"Do you realize that not everybody is healed? How would you feel if nothing were to happen here today?"

"I'd be disappointed but not surprised. I'm not sure if it's God's will that I be healed." Lynette was completely honest with Dr. White.

"How about you, Mrs. Cornelsen?"

"I believe God can heal Lynette, but I feel as she does, that I'd be disappointed but not surprised. I'm not sure that it is God's will for her to be healed." I was surprised I could be that open, but I didn't confess I actually doubted that a healing would take place. Would my lack of faith interfere?

"Let me explain a few things before I begin. In my ministry I have seen many healings. I would say up to 65 percent of the people I have prayed over have been healed. However, for some reason, 35 percent have not. It is always God's will that people should be well, but for some reason that we humans cannot understand, He sometimes chooses not to heal, as in Paul's case in the Bible."

"Perhaps you're also wondering if you have enough faith to be healed. Let me read to you about the healing of the woman who was plagued with a hemorrhage for 12 years.

> She had suffered much from many doctors through the years and had become poor from paying them and was no better but, in fact, was worse. She had heard all about the wonderful miracles Jesus did, and that is why she came up behind him through the crowd and touched his clothes.
>
> For she thought to herself, "If I can just touch his clothing, I will be healed." And sure

enough, as soon as she had touched him, the bleeding stopped and she knew she was well!

Jesus realized at once that healing power had gone out from him, so he turned around in the crowd and asked, "Who touched my clothes?"

His disciples said to him, "All this crowd pressing around you, and you ask who touched you?"

But he kept on looking around to see who it was who had done it. Then the frightened woman, trembling at the realization of what had happened to her, came and fell at his feet and told Him what she had done. And he said to her, "Daughter, your faith has made you well; go in peace, healed of your disease." Mark 5:26

"Lynette, your faith in Jesus was great enough for you to come for healing. I believe you have enough faith. Now relax and let the Holy Spirit do His work as I pray."

We gathered around, touching Lynette lightly. Dr. White laid his hands on her head. He began to pray, simply, and yet with power. Although he prayed humbly, he spoke with the authority of a child of God. He commanded any evil powers to leave and asked, even begged, God to heal Lynette.

"Are you beginning to feel anything, Lynette?"

"No, but I'm trying!"

"You don't have to try, Lynette. Relax. I know the Holy Spirit is present. The heat in the room indicates His presence. Let's continue our prayers."

I was uncomfortably warm. I had thought it was the sun shining in the window, but now I realized it was cloudy outside.

"My cheek is tingling," Lynette said hopefully.

Dr. White prayed for about a half-hour and then we sat down.

There had not been an instantaneous healing, but Dr. White was in no hurry.

"Let's talk for a while. Do you have any questions?" he asked.

"I have a question that's been on my mind for some time. Do you think it's possible that the devil has picked out our family to harass and try to destroy?" There. It was out. I wasn't aware until now that I was even harboring the thought!

"Tell me about your problems," he invited.

I had been weeping since the moment we stepped into his room and could hardly speak even now.

When I finished, he said, "I think there are more people in here who need to be prayed for."

"Yes, please pray for me. I'm sure I need emotional healing," I answered.

And so it was that everyone gathered around me as Dr. White prayed for me and our family. Above all, Dr. White asked God to give us peace in the midst of all our troubles. He especially prayed for peace of mind and heart for Lynette if she should not receive complete physical healing.

I had experienced the peace of God before, but never like I did that day. It truly was more wonderful than the human mind can understand. Upon our leavetaking, Dr. White advised us of the vital importance of our church continuing to pray for Lynette's healing. Alvin and Adina promised to look after that.

I wondered how Lynette would react. She had been so deeply disappointed last time. Would she be able to handle her frustrated hopes a second time?

"Yes, I guess I'm disappointed, but somehow I don't feel so depressed about it. I do feel a little something in my cheek, but I'm relaxed about it. I have complete peace right now that whatever happens, I am in God's will." Lynette slept peacefully all night. She never asked for healing again, but frequently she asked us to pray for peace. We would need it in the days just ahead.

Chapter Twenty-two

VALLEY OF SHADOWS

As the summer drew to a close, it brought with it the usual rush of changes. Harvest time for the farmers, school for the children, back-to-work for the vacationers. Bev had to return to Calgary, so my sister, Nita, offered to help me.

Cam, having weathered a rough summer, decided to start his search for a mother for his little boy. In his loneliness, he longed for a close friend, yet he resisted the thought of an intimate relationship. Several young girls had made some obvious moves in his direction, but he had not been interested.

Shortly after Janet's death, Cam had told us of a certain girl he had dreamt about, and whom he believed God was telling him to marry.

"But I'm not going to take out any girl for at least three months. I'm not going to remarry in a hurry. I want to be sure I love her and that I'll be really happy at my wedding," Cam told us.

When Cam did start dating, he took out several different girls but usually came home depressed.

"They're all nice," he said helplessly, "but I miss Janet!"

I had to be careful not to pressure him too much, yet I was anxious for Curtis to get a new mother soon, not only because it was so difficult for me, but also out of a very pragmatic consideration. Any girl would love to mother this adorable child. A year from now he might be a real terror, especially after I had spoiled him that long!

Lynette's health was deteriorating rapidly, and she needed almost constant assistance. I began to inquire as to how best to care for her should she become totally bedridden. Her wasting body was still too heavy for me to handle. It became extremely taxing to look after both Lynette and Curtis, especially as both slept less and less every night.

Lynette had contacted a touch of pneumonia in August, necessitating a suction machine to clear her breathing passages at night. The pain in her neck and shoulders became so severe that we kept increasing the strength of her painkillers. Was it possible that Curtis slept so fitfully because he sensed the mounting tensions? He loved to climb into Lynette's bed in the morning and play a game that he had invented for them. Each would clasp a hand of the other, then with the free hand grab hold of a bed post. They would count to ten together, and then clap their hands. The two of them had a loving understanding that needed few words and was beautiful to see.

During this time, our friend, Melvin Dueck, became very ill and was hospitalized for the last time. We visited him many times during the month that he lay hanging on to life by a mere thread. One day Art and I were called in. When we got to his bedside, Melvin grabbed my hand and tried to talk.

"Don't bother talking. Just relax." I told him.

"I love you guys. Tell Lynette I love her too!" he gasped.

"Thank-you, Melvin. We love you, too," I told him. I held his hand for a while and then joined Anne in the lounge.

She had been holding up very well, but long hours at the hospital, including a round-the-clock vigil the last week, was beginning to wear her down. Her children were there too and also weary-looking. How was it possible to watch a husband and father suffer so intensely, interminably waiting for death to relieve him?

"Oh, Lord, why must it hurt so much?" I prayed.

"Help them all," was my plea again.

Melvin fell asleep and breathed his last the next day. We were all relieved but keenly felt his absence when we went to the Dueck home. His funeral was scheduled for a few days later, October 7. The weather proved to be highly inclement. An unseasonal Manitoba blizzard hit our area, making the roads almost totally impassable. However, the memorial service was beautiful and challenging, well befitting the man who had borne his own sufferings cheerfully and who had dedicated his life to helping others. We were always to remember Melvin with a tender fondness.

That evening a friend of Lynette's stopped by to see her. They had been at Bible college together and a close friendship had developed. He had frequently visited her at the hospital, usually bringing one of his brothers with him. Because he and a brother of his had been in Africa for six months, Lynette had seen less of him this past year.

Although Lynette did not feel well enough to get out of bed, she was delighted to see her friend. I left them alone and went to the kitchen to catch up on some housekeeping. Although Lynette had a weak voice, I could frequently hear her laughing from the other end of the house. Lynette was having a great time. To hear her laugh was a wonderful treat to my ears.

The snow was still coming down and as the time grew late, I wondered whether the fellow was aware of the weather conditions.

"I'll be all right," he assured me as he left.

Lynette was in good spirits and talked gaily as I prepared her for bed. After massaging her neck and shoulders, I prayed with her. She lay back, closed her eyes, and said softly, "You know, Mom, I could have loved a guy like that!" She gave a big sigh and said, "I guess I'll never be able to marry!"

What could I say? I longed to assure her that her day would come but all I could manage was, "We'll have to wait and see about that." Inwardly I prayed, "Lord, you'll have to comfort her, I can't just now. I need your comfort too. Oh, help us all."

Immediately a picture formed in my mind. I saw Lynette dressed in white, walking through a white gate toward a man also dressed in white who was waiting to meet her with outstretched arms. Jesus was waiting to be her Bridegroom!

One Sunday evening in late October, I sensed a heavy depression settling on Lynette. She had spent the entire day in bed and was tired and bored. None of her friends had dropped in to alleviate her loneliness. Curtis had kept me busy so that I had neglected her somewhat.

My sister happened to stop by and she sized up the situation very quickly.

"Rose, you go and sit with Lynette while I occupy Curtis. Some day you'll be sorry you didn't take more time for her."

I was deeply touched by her thoughtfulness. I hadn't even thought of my need from that perspective, but I quickly took advantage of her offer.

Sitting on the edge of her bed, I asked Lynette if there was anything special she wanted to talk about.

"Yes, Mom, there is. I'm so scared to die," she said. She was forever shocking me by speaking so abruptly.

"That's normal, Lynette; everybody is afraid of dying. I guess we're afraid of the unknown. If we knew exactly what it was like, we'd probably not fear it so much."

"Maybe, but that's not much comfort when you're getting sicker every day and there's no hope of getting better," Lynette said reasonably.

"Would it help if I read to you about what heaven is like and you could think about the positive hope that you have in Jesus?" I asked, holding her trembling hand.

"I don't know. I wish you'd sing for me. I haven't been able to go to church for a month and I miss the singing so much. Would you sing "The Wonder of it All!" for me?" Lynette begged in her whisper as she quickly dabbed at her eyes.

She showed me where she kept her church hymnal and told me the page number of her favorite song. Somehow I was able to sing through that one and another and another, continuing for about an hour. I sang songs about our saving faith in Jesus, about the strengths and victories we have in Him, about Jesus' love, about heaven and its beauties. Sometimes my tears drowned out the words, but between Lynette and me there was a perfect joining of spirits, a communion that was wrought by the Holy Spirit. Could there actually be joy in the midst of grief?

Usually when Lynette asked us to have devotions with her, she'd ask us to pray for her. Tonight I asked her to pray first.

"Dear Lord," she whispered huskily, "Thank-you for loving me and helping me when I'm afraid. I want so much to get well, but tonight I want to tell You that I do want to submit to whatever Your will is for me. Thank-you for giving me peace. Amen."

It was my turn to pray.

"Thank-you, Lord, for giving Lynette to us. She has been such a blessing, such an example in love, peace, patience, and courage. Please continue to give her peace and grace in the days to come. Amen."

Chapter Twenty-Three

HOME WHERE I BELONG

"I'm going home where I belong," sang the Imperials on the car tape-deck.

The four of us were listening, each one in deep thought.

"Would you play that song at my funeral?" Lynette asked as the last notes ended.

Cam had offered to drive Lynette to the hospital that morning, the first Sunday in November. She had been gasping for air all night and finally consented to being admitted to the hospital in nearby Morris. A week earlier she had refused to discuss palliative care at the St. Boniface Hospital.

"You mean I'd have dying people all around me? Have the doctors given up on me? Well, I haven't. I'm going to show them I can lick this yet," she had said very determinedly.

Art was happy with her optimism, but I was surprised and less than pleased. I thought Lynette had accepted her condition as terminal. Obviously she was blocking out what she had known.

She had agreed to go into the Morris Hospital now only on condition that she could return home again.

"As soon as you're well enough, you will certainly come home again," I promised.

The following days were the most difficult of my life. I knew that God would have to sustain me if His promises were trustworthy at all. It was impossible for me to see my way through, but I resolved to forget about my feelings and attempt to make Lynette comfortable. A close friend of the family looked after Curtis most of the time, so I was free to stay in the hospital.

On Tuesday night, a friend came to visit. She brought Lynette a lovely flower arrangement. When she left, Lynette whispered, "Tell Cam to marry her. I believe God has chosen Pam for him. She is such a beautiful Christian. And she'd make a super mother for Curtis."

The next morning I noticed Lynette's fingernails were taking on a bluish tinge. Alarmed, I asked the doctor what that signified.

"Lack of oxygen. Perhaps you should call your husband and anybody else who should be here. Just in case."

I made only one phone call, but soon a parade of family members and friends began coming by. I was amazed again at the great impact Lynette had made on so many people. It was heartbreaking when the young man, her friend from OBI, came out of her room, put his arms around me, and cried like a child. Her closest cousin and best friend, Laurie, spent a few minutes alone with Lynette to say good-bye. I was also touched by the mature love and compassion shown by other cousins and friends her age. Several of them came to sit and hold her hand.

Art and I were given beds at the hospital so we could stay nearby. We slept fitfully until 4:00 a.m., when Lynette called for me. Fever was burning her up, her pain was intense, breathing was difficult, and she needed constant suctioning to clear her throat. She was so miserable!

"Mom, I'm so tired and I want to go home, but I'm scared!"

I pressed her hand.

"It's OK, Lynette. Just relax and go on home. Jesus is waiting for you. I'd go with you if I could and I'll be here as long as you need me, but when you leave me Jesus will be there. You'll find that He is no stranger to you. He loves you more than I do, and you know that must be a whole lot."

"Oh Lord, how can I say good-bye?" I breathed a silent prayer.

We read the "Daily Bread" devotional for the day as well as Scripture portions relating to heaven, and Psalm 23 on how

Jesus would be with her through the valley of death. At 6:00, Art came. He prayed with Lynette, and she calmed down. At 9:00, she was given a strong dose of morphine and she fell into a relaxed sleep. By noon we realized she wasn't going to wake up.

At 9:30 p.m., about 30 people gathered around her bed as she gently, quietly breathed her last. Pastor Stan prayed softly as her soul winged its way heavenward.

Thank-you, Lord!

We went home and slept quite peacefully. God had graciously sustained us. His promises were trustworthy.

Peace that passes understanding, truly!

The funeral was beautiful and peaceful. The winter weather was settling in, and that evening the snow fell, covering our girls' graves with a soft, white blanket. What a beautiful benediction!

It was November 7, 1985, exactly six months after Janet's death on May 7. Another answered prayer.

"Thank-you, Father God."

Chapter Twenty-Four

NEW BEGINNINGS

The roaring of the oceans waves did not entirely muffle the happy shouts of children romping on the sandy beach. I drifted into a state of euphoria, reveling in the luxury of basking in the hot sun on a beach in Miami, Florida.

"I could live like this forever," I thought and then screamed as I was suddenly doused with a bucket of chilly brine.

"You trying to turn yourself into a lobster, or what?" Art asked teasingly.

"Where did you come from? Can't I have a little peace for one afternoon?" I responded with mock indignation. I grabbed a handful of sand and threatened to throw it at him.

"You throw that at me and I'll drag you into the ocean."

"You would, too. How was the egg throwing contest? There was quite a crowd out there. Did you and Arlene have a chance to win?" I asked.

"We might have had if Cam hadn't picked such a good partner. They came in first. It was a lot of fun. You should have seen Arlene spattered with egg yolk!" Art said.

"It's so good to see Cam and Arlene having so much fun out here. It's hard to believe tonight is New Year's Eve. Too bad we have to leave tomorrow. I could handle another week of this." I sighed. This holiday had been a dream come true.

After Lynette's funeral, we had attempted to bring our home life back to a more normal condition. We were all emotionally drained and tried not to think about all the happenings of the past year. Curtis had seemed to become even more hyperactive and consumed most of my energies as well as his own.

"I dread to think of Christmas this year. Do you think there's a way to escape it?" I asked Art one day.

"Why don't we dig up our savings and take off for Florida? We'll never need it more than right now," Art suggested.

"We'll have to check with Cam and Arlene. We couldn't leave them home. Or Curtis — would we take him?" I wondered.

Arlene was exuberant at the prospect of the trip. Cam, now dating Pam quite regularly, was a bit hesitant at leaving her for the holiday season, but he also dreaded having to face a traditional Christmas at home with all its memories. So we compromised. Art, Arlene, and I drove by car, while Cam flew out on Boxing Day to Tampa, where we picked him up. Florence Loewen, a friend who frequently kept Curtis, offered to keep him till we got back.

During the long three-day drive each way, we had ample time to talk, both seriously and nonsensically. Arlene thrived on the attention she was getting, and began to confide in us freely. She told us about her grief, loneliness, doubts, and temptations. She revealed how she struggled to understand what God was expecting of her.

She longed to turn back the clock, she confided, to when she would crawl into Lynette's bed and share sisterly confidences with her. Arlene was a much more sensitive and deeply caring person than we had realized. Although she had understood our preoccupation with Lynette, she had suffered despair from feeling deserted throughout her high school years. She also revealed the loss of some close friendships at school after attending the previous year's New Year's Eve party.

At one point she said, "This trip has helped me to see that I have to make up my own mind about what I want to do with my future. I don't have to have my friends' approval to follow the Lord. I'm going to stand on my own two feet!"

"Just what do you mean by that?" I asked.

"I believe God wants me to prove my faith in Him by being obedient and taking water baptism. I'm going to go for it!" Arlene was very earnest in her decision.

"Oh, Arlene, you don't know how happy it makes me to hear you talk like that!" I said sincerely.

"I'm very proud of you, Arlene. You've matured so much over the past months, I'm sure you're going to make it," Art said with deep feeling.

We returned home from our holiday with renewed anticipation for the future. Although Cam would still occasionally find himself wracked with grief, he was also building a beautiful relationship with Pam. Quiet, soft-spoken, Pam was brimming with the love, compassion, patience and kindness that Cam needed so desperately. Her love for children was evident in the way she welcomed Curtis to accompany them on their dates.

Pam worked as a hairdresser in a downtown Winnipeg salon. Frequently, on her days off, she'd pick Curtis up and take him home with her. For Curtis, it had been love at first sight! A ride with Pam was always a happy adventure for him.

Our flickering hope was growing into a brighter, steadier flame. We would surely find a happy tomorrow yet!

Chapter Twenty-Five

BETTER TOMORROWS

It was Sunday morning, November 9,1986.

The howling blizzard had let up somewhat after dumping several feet of wet snow over all of southern Manitoba.

Cabin fever had set in on the wedding guests at our house. We listened to the cancellation announcements on the radio. Dozens of churches would have no services this morning. Driving had come to almost a complete standstill, and visibility was still near zero in unsheltered areas.

"The wedding of Cam Cornelsen and Pam Thiessen scheduled for this afternoon, will be postponed until Tuesday, November 11, same time, same place. . . ."

I glanced over to see Cam's reaction to the radio announcement. Earlier in the day he had shoveled his way off the yard, picked up Pam, and brought her over for dinner. The decision to delay the wedding had been extremely frustrating to everybody, but it was obviously the only answer to our dilemma.

Standing arm-in-arm in the middle of the kitchen, Cam swung Pam in a waltzing step, placed a deliberately slow kiss on her lips and said accusingly as though Pam had been personally responsible for the storm, "And to think we could have been man and wife by now. Aren't you sorry at all?"

I sighed.

Wedding plans had to be changed, but I was content.

We were entering a new phase of life. Cam's happiness brought cheer to all of us as he basked in the warmth of new-found love. Pam's sparkling eyes bespoke her own joy and her excitement. And as she generously gave her heart to Curtis, my own heart sang. I would miss Curtis desperately, but even that would be all right.

I breathed a quick prayer of thanksgiving as I prepared the fruit salad for our meal.

"O Father, How can I thank You sufficiently for Your gracious kindness to my family? Your love overwhelms me when I think of how You have helped us and answered our prayers for Cam and Curtis. Their home will be complete. Thank-you.

. . . .

Eight months later, on July 13, 1987, the phone rang.

"A collect call from Arlene. Will you accept the charges?" The operator spoke with a heavy accent.

"Of course!" I said eagerly. "Arlene, where are you?"

"Hi, Mom! I'm calling from Austria. How are you?"

Arlene had responded to God's call for summer missionary service in Europe. It had been a real step of faith for her to leave home again after a year away at Bible college. It was wonderful to hear her voice after two weeks.

"So what are you doing there?" I asked.

"Handing out Christian literature and just befriending local people, hoping to get them interested in the gospel. It's pretty hard though, because I don't know the German language too well. And I'm so homesick!"

"Are you sorry you went?"

"Oh no, Mom, I'm learning so much. I'm learning to depend on God all the time. It's all so strange. New people, new language, new surroundings. We even depend on donations for our food. Just pray that God will carry me through this summer." Arlene was learning fast.

Thank-you, Lord!

. . . .

A Christian singles' club of Winnipeg invited me to share my story at their annual spring banquet. Upon finishing my talk, in which I related the anecdote of "The Footprints in the Sand," and what it had meant to us, the soloist got up to sing. Rhonda McRorie and I had never met, but we knew it was no coincidence that she had chosen to sing "Footprints," that evening. She had composed her own lyrics and music, providing a profound closing for the program. We sensed God had brought us together for a purpose.

Rhonda told me of a dream she had of producing a musical drama based on the theme of "Footprints." She had written several songs already but needed a storyline to pull it all together.

A year and a half later, Rhonda's dream became a reality when the drama, "Better Tomorrows," was performed by a talented group of Christian actors on stage at the Mennonite Brethren Bible College. It was with mixed emotions of sadness and elation that our family watched our own lives reenacted. With deep gratitude we realized again how merciful and kind God was to carry us through such dark turmoil and then light up our lives with such peace, hope and joy.

. . . .

Another year passed. A tiny blue-blanketed bundle of joy has entered Cam and Pam's home. He will answer to the name, Craig Arthur Scott.

"No way," four-year-old Curtis vehemently disagrees. "My brother's name is Rainbow."

"Why?"

"I don't know. It's just Rainbow."

We will never know where Curtis picked up the name but to the family it is a promise from God for better tomorrows!

. . . .

The long shadows of the tall pines vanished as darkness gently gathered them up. Art and I had thoroughly enjoyed a week of holidays at the lake, but it was time to go home. In farewell, we hiked down to the waterfall, climbed up some rocks and watched the sun set. As the light failed, we sat on the moss-covered rock, marvelling at the haunting beauty of our surroundings.

Art wrapped me in his strong arms and lifted his voice in praise to God.

"Lord, we can only thank You and praise You for Your grace and goodness to us. Thank-you for letting us experience all this beauty around us. Please continue to work in our lives as we continue to depend on You to carry us through life."

Softly the moonlight filtered through the pines, placing a benediction on our heads.